Jan Dibbets

Essays by
R.H. Fuchs
M.M.M. Vos

with an introduction by
Martin Friedman

Jan Dibbets

Walker Art Center, Minneapolis

Rizzoli, New York

Published on the occasion of the exhibition
Jan Dibbets, organized by Walker Art Center
in association with the Stedelijk Van
Abbemuseum. Support for the exhibition
was provided by the National Endowment
for the Arts and KLM Royal Dutch Airlines.

Presentation of the exhibition in
Minneapolis was made possible in part by
The Bush Foundation, the Dayton Hudson
Foundation for Dayton's and Target
Stores, the General Mills Foundation, the
Honeywell Foundation, The McKnight
Foundation, the Minnesota State Arts Board
and The Pillsbury Company Foundation.

Library of Congress Cataloging
in Publication Data

Dibbets, Jan, 1941-
    Jan Dibbets: essays

    Catalogue of an exhibition.
    Bibliography: p. 148
    Includes index.
    1. Photography, Artistic—Exhibitions.
2. Dibbets, Jan, 1941-   —Exhibitions.
I. Fuchs, Rudolfo Herman, 1942-
II. Vos, M.M.M. III. Walker Art Center.
IV. Title.
TR647.D52 1987 779'.092'4 87-60503
ISBN 0-8478-0873-4 (Rizzoli)
ISBN 0-935640-24-X (pbk.)

Trade edition first published in the United
States of America in 1987 by Rizzoli
International Publications, Inc., 597 Fifth
Avenue, New York, NY 10017.

Copyright © 1987 Walker Art Center
All rights reserved.

No part of this publication may be repro-
duced in any manner whatsoever
without permission in writing by Walker
Art Center.

Designed by Jeffrey Cohen.
Printed and bound in West Germany.

Dimensions are in inches and centimeters;
height precedes width precedes depth.

(cover)
Spoleto Self-Portrait 1981
color photographs and
pencil on cardboard, two parts
28¾ x 28¾ each
73 x 73
Private collection

(frontispiece)
Cupola 1985–1986
color photographs, watercolor and pencil
on paper mounted on chipboard
72½ x 72½
184 x 184
Private collection

Contents

Perspective Correction,
Big Square 1968
black and white photograph
on photographic canvas
43¼ x 43¼
110 x 110
Private collection

Perspective Unlimited

Martin Friedman

The spacious studio where Jan Dibbets produces his interpretations of landscape and architectural themes is located in a district known as Amsterdam East. This relatively bland area of red-brick buildings was a thriving Jewish quarter before World War II and the center of the city's diamond cutting industry; today, Holland's vastly reduced Jewish population is scattered elsewhere throughout the city. During the bleak, rainy December afternoon last year when Dibbets and I met to discuss his exhibition and its catalogue, the streets were quiet except for the squawks of large black and white magpies making their awkward flight from bare tree branches to the moss-covered roof of the neighborhood landmark, a 1923 multi-tiered, circular public bathhouse visible from the studio window.

One could reasonably expect the maker of carefully ordered compositions to reflect these precise qualities in his own persona, but this is hardly the case. Dibbets is the essence of amiable informality; he is of medium height, his sandy hair is a bit unruly, and sartorially he is somewhat rumpled. His conversation is lively and voluble, revealing a broad awareness and curiosity about what's going on in European and American art, and the world in general. For all the clarity of his work, he is not above self-doubt and frequently abandons an idea that seemed to be coming along nicely. Occasionally when things aren't going too well with a project, he seeks refuge in cooking, retreating to his commodious kitchen to concoct a meal for a few friends.

Given that Amsterdam is one of the most densely populated cities in Europe, the spaciousness of Dibbets's studio and residence, which occupy two floors of a three-story structure, is an anomaly. The building's transformation from drapery factory to artist's quarters required tearing out numerous partitions. Now its loftlike top floor serves as a pied-à-terre and exhibition space for the Dutch collector Frits Becht, Dibbets's partner in acquiring and recycling the building. On the ground floor is a large studio where Dibbets adheres his photographic prints to white chipboard surfaces, embedding these in networks of graphite and wax crayon perspectival lines. This area also houses a darkroom for processing the film that Dibbets shoots a few times a year of landscapes, sea vistas and building interiors—recurring images in his compositions. Leaning against the studio walls during my visit were a few works in progress—large square-shaped pictures based on architectural interiors ranging from the fresco-adorned dome of a Tuscan church to the concentric circles of the Guggenheim Museum's glass skylight.

In the second floor reception area of Dibbets's building, a few arresting examples of early twentieth-century Dutch furniture, European cut-glass vases of the 1920s and 30s, masks and figures from what was once Dutch New Guinea, and works by such contemporary Minimalist stalwarts as Carl Andre, Robert Ryman, Sol LeWitt and Robert Mangold are, from time to time, casually deployed. And in this airy space several work tables are piled high with books and catalogues of recent European and American painting and sculpture exhibitions.

Though his collection of early twentieth-century Dutch design is more the result of numerous happy accidents than of systematic accretion, Dibbets has a particular eye for Amsterdam School furniture designed by vanguard architects. A prize trophy of his enterprising foraging in local antique shops and flea markets is a strongly sculptural 1917 dark wood table designed by Piet Kramer; its ponderous udderlike forms predict the transition from Art Nouveau's sinuous line to Art Deco angularity. Closely related stylistically are other treasures of the period: a few elegant wooden armchairs, a step-sided 1903 chaise longue example of Dutch Art Noveau, and a florid Art Moderne rug that once graced Amsterdam's legendary Tuchinsky Theater, a movie palace without equal, Dibbets maintains, in the whole of Europe.

Off the second floor reception area is a library furnished with a pair of 1950s gray upholstered couches and two side chairs, late designs of Gerrit Rietveld, the legendary De Stijl architect. These offer fascinating contrast to an earlier example of Rietveld's design sensibility that Dibbets has also acquired for his collection: a faithful line-by-line copy of the architect's celebrated 1923 Berlin Chair composed of black, white and gray rectangular wooden planes.

Though Dibbets admires the works of many of his contemporaries, the primary shaping forces of his art, he says, are historical. Especially influential was his early discovery of the accomplishments of nineteenth-century architecture and engineering. A grant from the British Arts Council in 1966 provided him with a year of study at London's St. Martin's School of Art, where he soon found himself spending more time in the library than in the painting studio.

There he pored over books of illustrations and studied detailed working drawings of the daring, space-defying industrial structures conceived by visionary engineers of the Victorian era, for whom the use of steel became a high art form. He was fascinated by the work of Joseph Paxton, whose crowning achievement was the 1851 Crystal Palace, and enthralled by the genius of Isambard Kingdom Brunel, the exotically named Portsmouth-based civil engineer whose dramatic tensile structures include the Royal Albert bridge and the cavernous volumes of Paddington Station.

But for all his absorption with the marvels of engineering, Dibbets also attributes his aesthetic ancestry to more conventional artistic sources. As a student, he came under the spells of Giotto and Pierro della Francesca, whose flatly-painted hieratic figures, elegantly positioned within simple architectural frameworks, represented the essence of pure architectonic form. He remains susceptible to the crystalline imagery of Jan Vermeer, that master equilibrist of light, color and space. And less celebrated than Vermeer's, the imagery of another seventeenth-century Dutch painter, Pieter Janszoon Saenredam, continues to serve Dibbets as a touchstone. In luminous church interiors of Saenredam, actual and imagined architectural elements are synthesized in richly orchestrated compositions that are distinguished by meticulous delineation.

A more immediate shaping force has been the gravitational pull of Piet Mondrian and the De Stijl movement of the early twentieth century. In the lingua franca of De Stijl, forms of the material world were transmuted into spiritualized essence symbolized by grids of vertical and horizontal lines, and planes of pure color. "A single painting by Mondrian," says Dibbets, "dominates a wall, and even his smallest canvas can suggest limitless space."

But for all his admiration of De Stijl's reductive purity, Dibbets is no recapitulator of its theoretical or visual maxims. Not only is recognizable subject matter always present in his art, but so is a quality of specific locale, a fact especially evident in his interpretations of architectural subject matter. And, unlike the De Stijl artists, in whose work time was virtually suspended, Dibbets deals with its passage. In this regard, he is closer to the Cubists: within a Dibbets work, the subject is perceived simultaneously from various angles and under changing conditions of light.

Although other contemporary artists whose work interests him include the American Minimalists, he points out that his tastes go beyond purist phenomena. They include, he says, the quirky, anatomically-derived imagery of Bruce Nauman, Mario Merz's metaphysical spirals based on mathematical progressions found in nature, and the myth-charged imagery of Joseph Beuys.

Dibbets's work is sometimes compared to that of Richard Long, who makes three-dimensional circular and linear rock configurations, some of which he records in serial photographs. He greatly respects Long's attitudes but considers himself to be less involved with Conceptual Art or Earth Art ideas.

Doubtless, the resistance of Dibbets's work to easy categorization has contributed to its somewhat enigmatic status in the international art world. He came on the scene in the mid-1960s along with a number of other European and American artists looking for new ways to express time and space. From his early series of Perspective Corrections he moved on to revealing many aspects of a subject by photographing sections of it from a fixed position, then combining the images on a white surface. Still, no matter how systematic his approach, more emanates from these closeups and panoramic views of nature than mastery of process. Though they retain strong descriptive qualities, these are fundamentally Dibbets's meditations on the indeterminate character of light and space. For example, in his complex faceted impressions of landscapes, the horizon lines are both near and infinitely distant. Whether evoking endless space in landscape studies, or focusing on objects near at hand, such as the gleaming surface of an automobile or the radial configurations of gray concrete pavement, his concern is to reveal clear underlying structure in the natural and man-made worlds.

Dibbets's summers are spent in San Casciano dei Bagni, a remote Tuscan village near the Umbrian border where he owns a small house. There he works on studies for larger compositions to be realized on return to Holland. Currently, he is absorbed with themes that contain aspects of his early closeup and panoramic studies. Recent subjects include the high-domed ceilings of old Romanesque churches and other monumentally scaled structures. Through accretions of photographic impressions that explore their intricate geometry, Dibbets reveals their formal logic.

Though his free-form compositions are not confined to ecclesiastical subjects, their presence raises a few questions. Is this Dibbets's latter day variation on a thematic idea that obsessed one of his idols, Saenredam? Or does it go further and have some particular spiritual significance for him? Indeed, whether his absorption with church architecture is anything more than a desire to reveal its underlying order is not clear even to Dibbets. Though raised a Roman Catholic in the southern Dutch village of Weert, he professes no particular interest in formal religion, and his objective, he says, is to express the "theology of order," rather than that of any established faith. Nevertheless, his primal circles and spirals of "deconstructed" architectural elements are reminiscent of ancient ritualistic symbols as well as mysterious astral orbs made visible through the high resolution photography of space satellites.

Discussing his use of circles, Dibbets recalls his early fascination with megalithic religious sites that are scattered throughout the countryside of Wales and southern England. To some, he understands, the whirling domes that are such a large part of his recent work suggest nebulaelike masses afloat in outer space. When this idea came up in our conversation, he suddenly produced a stack of books that were filled with vividly colored NASA satellite photographs of planets and of the earth as observed from the surface of the moon.

Given that background, to regard Dibbets's works solely as essays in pure form is to misunderstand their premise. His art has another, more romantic aspect, well beyond revealing underlying structures of forms in nature and the man-made world. Indeed, through his subtle wizardry, these forms are transmuted into atmospheric shapes that exist within a cosmos of his own invention.

**Perspective Correction,
My Studio II, 3: Square with
Cross on Floor** 1969
black and white photograph
on photographic canvas
47¼ x 47¼
120 x 120
Private collection

On Photography and the Art of Jan Dibbets

M.M.M. Vos

Few artists in this century have reflected so deeply on the nature and possibilities of photography as Jan Dibbets, and yet to call him a photographer would be misleading. Although he uses photography in the execution of his works, for Dibbets, a photograph is not a final product but a medium—one with specific properties, of course, but nonetheless a medium, just as paint is a medium for the painter and not an end product. Between this attitude and the photographer's conception of the photograph as final product yawns a gulf far wider and deeper than is commonly assumed.

The old and for the most part futile discussion about art versus photography appears to have fallen silent, with more and more people taking photography for granted as an independent art form. And there is little wrong with that, for what constitutes art is as problematical as ever and, on the rational level at least, largely a matter of definition. But even if photography is taken to be an art form in its own right, the question still remains whether that particular form has anything to do with visual art in the strict sense.

Problems arise when, having affirmed the independence of photographs by rejecting as misleading all comparison with drawing and painting, they are nonetheless presented, interpreted and criticized in the context of those art forms. The very comparison that we had agreed to avoid reimposes itself when we resort to the use of terms and criteria derived from painting. The misunderstanding that arises from this is not only great but also bears a striking resemblance to an old misconception in painting, namely that painting and representation are synonymous, that the representation is the painting and the painting the representation. Good painters have always recognized this fallacy; and contrary to what is so often seen in contemporary iconology, they never fail to make a careful distinction between the represented object and the presented form. Admittedly, the problem of *imitatio naturae* has been a recurrent subject of discussion since the Italian Renaissance, but at crucial moments—as soon as the following of nature assumed a slavish and purely technical form—artists have been quick to make a plea for creation and interpretation, idea and imaginative portrayal.

The invention of photography drove a wedge between painting and representation. Artists gradually stopped being the purveyors of representation, and increasingly became the makers of free art. Imagination went off in a different direction, so to speak, thereby paving the way for the non-representational art of this century.

Paradoxically, writers on photography have, perhaps unconsciously, maintained the old misunderstanding about representation in their efforts to find criteria for determining the artistic merits of a photograph in its representational quality. This tendency is also common among photographers themselves. With mild exaggeration one could state that the consequence of this preoccupation with representation is that virtually all photographers overlook the medium itself, in the sense that, in terms of art, they only partially recognize the implications of the nature of the photographic process and the specific workings of the camera. There is nothing wrong with that so long as photography serves the purpose of producing pictures of objects (the importance of which, from a cultural and historical viewpoint, can hardly be overestimated). Art, however, has different aims.

Dibbets started as a painter, and he does not conceal the fact that when he uses photography, he does so in the traditions of painting. The rigorous, yet subtle abstractions of Piet Mondrian, for example, and of such seventeenth-century Dutch masters as Pieter Saenredam and Jan Vermeer, are important to him. The characteristics and qualities of the so-called professional photograph are of secondary interest to him, because when he uses photography his objective is not to produce unique pictures, but to develop a way of seeing. The formal concepts he is concerned with are strictly conceived from the nature and possibilities of photography; furthermore the execution of his works hinges on a use of the camera that is often unconventional but no less legitimate for that. In this connection, some comments on the relationship between photography and reality may be of interest.

• •

One of the fundamental characteristics of the photographic image is its relationship to time, not experienced time, but mechanical time—the time of shutter and exposure. The length of exposure—the 1/1000 second, one minute, or even one day, as in Niepce's very first photographs in the last century—is of importance only in relation to the desired image. In the photographic process, the time of exposure is exclusively a factor of quantitative importance. We take this fact at face value, we hardly stop to think about it, certainly not when we look at photographs of relatively static things such as landscapes and buildings, crystals and planets. Time is more compellingly perceived, albeit in a frozen form, in photographs of moving objects, especially if those objects are people. Important in this connection is what has been called photography of "the decisive moment," that is to say, the photographic registration of unique and meaningful moments that would otherwise have been swallowed up in the stream of life. The master of this genre was the French photographer and painter Henri Cartier-Bresson.

"To me," Cartier-Bresson once observed, "photography is the simultaneous recognition, in a fraction of a second, of the significance of an event as well as of a precise organization of forms which give that event its proper expression."[1] This notion, which presupposes great flexibility of both body and mind, became widely dispersed through his *Images à la sauvette,* a book of photographs published in English in 1952 under the title *The Decisive Moment.*

Since then, countless photographers all over the world have been looking for that decisive moment every second of the day. Their cameras click ad infinitum and the pictures are distributed around the globe. Beautiful photographs, horrifying, moving and surprising photographs, but all of them photographs that, on close scrutiny, irrevocably lead to one and the same conclusion: someone was there, someone was alert, someone pressed the button at exactly the right moment. The importance of *who* that someone was pales next to the bare fact that *someone was there.* And the more often we look at a famous photograph the more anonymous the image becomes. The reasons for that anonymity undoubtedly lie in the nature of photography itself. For the causality of the photographic process has no fundamental connection with any decisive moment whatsoever. As far as the camera is concerned one moment is just as important as the next or, if one prefers, just as unimportant. But for the photographer who wants to say something with his photographs, the selection of the moment is of paramount importance.

Cartier-Bresson himself, incidentally, never concealed his skepticism about photography. In 1952, for instance, he wrote that photographers aim at something of far less durable value than painters. And that is the crux of the matter. It is precisely that ephemeral quality of the photograph, the impression of brevity, that pursues us in our dealings with photography. In everyday life we seldom stop to think about this because photographs, after all, serve all sorts of short-term purposes. But as soon as photographs are shown in a gallery or museum, their ephemeral quality is suddenly manifest. Even in the hands of the most expert professionals, photography hardly seems capable of representing more than the reflection of a fleeting and fleeing world view. Quite apart from the often intriguing photographs themselves, the oeuvre of any photographer evokes an image of an irreparably fragmented reality. Each photographic fragment is absorbed into its own isolation. At whatever point in the photographer's life it was made, it never has compelling consequences for subsequent photographs. All further possibilities remain open at all times; nowhere do we see a development of ideas, no progress, no regression, no movement at all. And that immobility, so to speak, accords perfectly with the one-dimensional relationship between time, photography and reality. The camera clicked, and that is in fact all, however inexorable it may sound.

With all due respect for the powers of observation of outstanding photographers such as Edward Weston, August Sander, André Kertész, Brassai, Diane Arbus, and many others, we cannot ignore the fact that the work of even the best photographer is permeated with a *quantitative* principle that is impossible to stem, let alone eliminate, by even the most stringent selection. The mechanical repetition that is inherent in each and every apparatus, and hence also in the camera, blocks experienced time, distorts history and hermetically seals each photograph in an eternal repetition of the *now,* regardless of whether that photograph was made today or a century ago.

To return to the problem of art and photography, surely everyone who dismisses the problem as outdated finds it remarkable that Cartier-Bresson himself referred to it repeatedly, implicitly but also explicitly. As he explained to Ferdinando Scianna, his late involvement in drawing and painting was due to his rediscovery of his original calling, and to finally closing the parentheses around photography.[2] André Pieyre de Mandiargues reacted to this by expressing the hope that the present concerns of his old friend Cartier-Bresson would not lead to the conclusion that painting takes priority over photography.[3] And finally, Yves Bonnefoy, the poet, commented that Cartier-Bresson brushed aside any praise for his photographs saying: "It's simply that I'm nervous, and that I love painting.

About photography I know nothing."[4] Considering Cartier-Bresson's lifelong preoccupation with photography, there is undoubtedly a touch of irony in such statements. Still, when a great photographer expresses himself in these terms it amounts to more than a mere subjective opinion. Quite apart from any thought of hierarchy in the arts, Cartier-Bresson's attitude calls for a renewed reflection on the difference between painting and photography.

If there is anything in visual art that plays an important role it is the question of beauty and ugliness, however changeable and complicated the meaning of those terms may be. When someone describes a certain photograph as beautiful—and beautiful photographs abound—then that simply means, from the viewpoint of art, that a photograph can also be ugly. Photographs can be technically imperfect, out of focus, or dull, misleading, in bad taste, superfluous, uninteresting, amateurish. But can they actually be ugly in the way things in our daily surroundings can be ugly: a shoe, a chair, a painting? I have my doubts, for in my opinion the most unsatisfactory photograph is still saved by the inexorableness of the photographic process, the magic of light and the phantom of the image. All conceivable shortcomings with respect to subject, form and technique are incapable of transforming the primary wonder of photography into something ugly. In other words, the copyright of the photographic image rests with nature itself, and nature takes no notice of man-made codes of beauty and ugliness. If we find certain photographs beautiful, then our judgment seldom has anything to do with the wonder of photography per se, but with circumstantial aspects relating to the meaning of form and representation.

The question of beauty and ugliness suddenly becomes acute in confrontation with photographs of horrifying events, especially if the photographed moment coincides with the most decisive moment in our lives: the moment of death. To concern oneself, when confronted with a photograph of a murder or an execution, with the question of whether the photograph is rhythmically beautiful or whether it has a balanced composition is, to put it mildly, bad form. Everyone senses immediately that the horror of the moment perverts the question of beauty or ugliness. But remarkably, with paintings of even the cruelest scenes, there is always room for an opinion about beauty or ugliness.

Aesthetic criteria—so difficult and yet fundamental in dealing with painting—are lost to photography as soon as death emerges on the scene. But if that is so, then we are justified in asking ourselves whether there is not some element of execution in every photograph, however innocent. Language at any rate points in that direction—think of the expression, "shooting a picture."

The profound relationship between photography and death is impressively described in Roland Barthes's last book *La chambre claire,* published just before his death in 1980.[5] Reflecting on photographs of his dead mother, Barthes writes that photography is tormented by the ghost of painting. But, he argues, photography is not an art but a form of magic, a magic that due to its bond with *time* and *death* has more affinity with the art of the theater than with that of painting. We are familiar, he continues, with the original relationship between the death cult and the theater. What we encounter in photographs is the motionless theater of death.

Perhaps Barthes was inspired to take this surprising turn in his thinking about art and photography by the film critic André Bazin, who once observed that photography does not create eternity, but *embalms* time.[6] How true those words and how strong the mummifying effect of photography are never more vividly experienced than when the projection of a film is suddenly stopped. Now many photographers are expert embalmers of time, but the underlying tragedy of professional photography surely lies in the fact that even the simplest Kodak snapshot mummifies.

• • •

This state of affairs does not detract in any way from the fact that photography, especially color photography, yields an awesome wealth of images of the everchanging appearance of nature. As such, photography has always been of interest to artists and has indeed influenced the development of visual art in more than one respect. The history of this influence has been quite thoroughly researched in recent years, in such books as *Art and Photography,* by Aaron Scharf. A very different problem presents itself when photography is used directly in visual art, in other words, when a painter like Dibbets seeks to incorporate the ephemeral nature of photography not only into his own subjectively experienced reality, but also into more objective ideas about art.

Dibbets once said that he wanted to "dress up what Mondrian had taken so much trouble to undress."[7] This statement not only clarifies his objective, it is also indicative of his attitude toward photography. What he is concerned with is to develop structural principles that will enable the sensory world of photography to enter the ideational world of abstract art. But to accomplish that, more is needed than conventional photography possesses in the way of aesthetic and expressive makeup. In the context of visual art, the effect of subtle lighting, an unusual angle, careful staging, a balanced composition, a dramatic contrast or a decisive moment is merely to gloss over the naked essence of the medium. Here the distance at once becomes obvious between the art of representation on the one hand and the art of "imaging" on the other. This distance is sometimes so great as to make each of the two arts appear to be rooted in a fundamentally separate mentality.

However that may be, on the phenomenological level, the photograph is a frame in a film, just as a film is a photograph moving in time. Only complete acceptance of this fact can lead to a more fundamental understanding of the creative possibilities of photography. Two closely connected problems appear to present themselves here. First, visual art, unlike music, for instance, unfolds its structures within the dimensions of space. So the question is how photography, with its causal connection with time and movement, can be transformed into structures that are bound to location and space (a problem incidentally that painters always encounter when seeking to express movement). Second, every photograph depicts something: abstract photographs do not, in fact, exist, because the photographic process always hinges on the fixation of light reflected by matter. What is depicted in the photograph can sometimes be difficult or impossible to identify, but that does not make it abstract. The problem then is how this singular power of representation can be countered.

Dibbets's concept shows convincingly, in my opinion, how photography can function as a valid medium of artistic imaging. Among the first works in which, after a period of abstract painting, he used photography are the Perspective Corrections of the late 1960s. These works are about the ambiguity of depth on a flat plane. The classical problem that painters have wrestled with, especially since the Italian Renaissance, is that of reconciling flatness and depth. On the one hand the space of one-point perspective offered human action a more or less dramatic form, while on the other hand every good painter realized that the ordering of things and occurrences in the third dimension maintained a certain tension with the ordering of form and color in the flat plane. Great painters were always masters in the solution of this conflict. Now the photograph, by its very nature, depicts space in one-point perspective. The illusion of this space is so strong that the plane of the photograph virtually disappears, which is unacceptable for the reality content of an art work. In Dibbets's Perspective Corrections, he cancels out one illusion with another, thereby making the photographic plane visible. Certain trapezoids, when photographed from a particular angle, appear as a square in the photographic plane. Its perspective distortion is corrected and the third dimension is restored to the plane. This correction is, compared with the curious anamorphoses of past centuries, irreversible. The anamorphosis still offers our eye the possibility of seeing through the distorted image: we can, after all, change our angle of vision. The photograph excludes this possibility. Our eye is shackled to the eye of the camera. But there is more. The same trapezoid drawn on a white sheet of paper would hardly look remarkable if it appeared as a square in a photograph. What we know would not contradict what we see. And that is exactly what happens in Dibbets's Perspective Corrections. From the oblique lines of the surroundings we conclude that the square must in fact be a different shape, but we cannot see it. The trapezoid imposes itself as a square in the plane of the photograph, or, more precisely, it dissociates itself from the photographed space, assumes an indeterminate, floating character, and slides like something out of an abstract world over the minutely detailed illusion of the photograph.

The importance of these Perspective Corrections for Dibbets's later work is obvious. Here he realized for the first time an idea within photography that transcends representation, as such. Especially in combination with sequential photography—which at that time had hardly been used since Eadweard Muybridge a century earlier—we can see how he develops further principles of abstraction.

Dibbets's sequential photographs are anticipated in *Shadows Taped off on a Wall* (1969; p. 28), a concept that was realized as an exhibition in Museum Haus Lange in Krefeld, Germany. (The piece itself survives only in the form of documentary installation photographs.) The contours of moving shadows were marked on the walls of the exhibition space at regular intervals. The resulting light-graphics captured a movement that we could never have perceived as a whole because of its slowness. Time and motion, with all the connotations of a planet turning around the sun, were thus transformed into space and location. The *succession* of invisible intervals in time became the *juxtaposition* of a structure limited by the dimensions of a concrete space.

This work originated in the atmosphere of conceptual art and—in accordance with the mentality of those days, which was concerned more with exploration than realization—there is still a fairly loose relationship between form and concept. But the idea of the movement of light assumed a more compelling form in works such as *The Shadows in My Studio* (1969; p. 29) and *The Shortest Day at the Van Abbemuseum* (1970; p. 30). Changes in the light were now directly recorded in photographs taken every ten minutes. The space in which the light moves is of no particular importance; it could in fact be any interior with a window. Consequently our attention is drawn all the more strongly to the light itself, which is after all the *conditio sine qua non* of photography. Many photographers attempt to arrange light in special ways, but light, or rather the lighting, in that case, serves merely to heighten an expressive effect in an image. At this point Dibbets, searching for causes and not for effects, dissociates the light from the image, as it were, by creating a sequence. The movement of pure light unfolds before our eyes in an abstract series, stationary and yet in motion, never previously perceived.

Dibbets's application of sequential photography implies not only an acceptance, but also and most significantly the utilization of the factor of repetition inherent in the camera. Technically speaking there is an additional factor: the photographic process actually only registers quantities of light, in a sense reducing the image to a random by-product. This state of affairs, as we have seen, offers little scope for the creativity of an artist. But with sequential photography the situation is entirely different. In a sequence our attention is immediately diverted from the image per se to the manner of depiction. Photography here suddenly seems to gain dimensions that raise it above the laws of cause and effect. Besides— and most importantly—the photo sequence offers a logical principle of form whereby photographs, which are by definition fragmentary, can be combined into structures that appeal to the imagination.

While *The Shortest Day at the Van Abbemuseum* shows us natural changes in the light viewed from a fixed camera position, in other works, such as the elusive Shutterspeed Pieces, Dibbets regulates the light by means of a technical feature of the camera. A single, simple motif is photographed with increasing shutter speed. In *Louverdrape, Vertical* (1971; p. 32), however, he simply uses the opening and closing of a window blind on the one hand to regulate the amount of light and, on the other, to bring about a visually intriguing merging of plane and depth. The sequence, consisting of sixty-five photographs, starts in darkness. The blind is closed. Slowly a pattern of lines emerges, successively growing clearer and lighter, out of the nothingness. The lines become wider, the patterns open up and, in the middle of the series, offer a view of a sun-drenched garden. After that the image again gradually closes up, regaining its abstraction, so to speak, and reverts to the darkness of the initial picture plane. The development of this movement in its entirety is embedded in a chain of light sequences and here again it is in fact the light, the immaterial light, that seems to operate independently in all its purity.

As regards the significance of the sequence as a structural principle, it is characteristic of Dibbets that he developed the Louverdrape series from a film of the same name, by printing the frames of the film as photographs. He adopted the same principle in *Film: Painting Black Vase,*

Horizontal (1972; p. 34), this time, however, by translating the movement of a film camera along a stationary motif into photographs that are then mounted, like a painting, in a rectangle. Generally speaking we have no difficulty, when watching a film, in interpreting camera movements as a moving angle of vision—so long as they are not too rapid. We can still see stationary things as stationary. But, in fact, the static world moves across a stationary field of projection. It is precisely this curious reversal, this basic phenomenon of film, that is Dibbets's concern in *Film: Painting Black Vase, Horizontal.* Eighty images of the vase are present simultaneously. We see the vase moving across the picture plane, but at the same time we know that it is not the vase that is moving but the camera. Our imagination does all it can to interpret the fixed rows of images as movement uninterrupted in time. The simultaneity, however, of all the moments prevents this and constantly redirects the movement back to its source. What we seem to perceive is perhaps not so much movement as the birth of movement.

Sequential photography and movement, camera position and ambiguity of space come together in a group of works on the theme of the Dutch horizon. In the Panoramas and Dutch Mountains, Universes and Comets, Dibbets makes the camera swing round on its own axis (sometimes obliquely to the earth, sometimes perpendicularly) with photographs being taken at intervals of the same number of degrees. The structure of the works that originate in this way lies not only in the structure of a sequence, but equally in the behavior of the horizon in the viewfinder. Dibbets's choice of motif for these works is—apart from a subjective affinity for the vastness of the Dutch landscape—easily explained when we realize that sea, air and lowland have a natural tendency, due to the small number of points of reference, to appear in the image in a decidedly frontal manner. Seen through the viewfinder, sea, air and land appear delimited as more or less abstract two-dimensional forms, however without the infinite space of the landscape being lost. Thus Dibbets is able to make the horizon function as a formal and at the same time poetic element in the structure of his work. He does not feel restricted by the position of the horizon, for the camera, after all, has no preferences. In reality we always see the horizon as horizontal, whichever way we turn and twist our heads. But the camera is unaffected by this constancy of perception. It has its own frame of reference—the viewfinder—which our eye obeys, and within which the horizon does not have a fixed position or direction. The viewfinder detaches the horizon from the earth, thereby allowing Dibbets to make this eminently Dutch motif move in an imaginary, or rather dreamed, space.

In this respect *0°–135° Horizontal* (1972; p. 96) and *Reconstruction*

Cross 0°–135° (1972–1973; p. 36) demonstrate the power of the frame of reference in a sober but forceful way. The camera turns around an axis perpendicular to a white wall, taking a photograph, every fifteen degrees, of a small black motif, a section of line or a cross. The tilting of the camera is to be seen in the sequence as a mysterious tilting of the motif. The visual idea, which is almost nakedly exposed in the coupling of motif and viewfinder, recurs—but now incorporated in the sensory magnificence of nature—in all the works in which the Dutch landscape is reconstructed within a cool geometric form concept. One of the last works from this period, *Big Comet 3°–60° Sky/Sea/Sky* (1973; p. 98) seems to provide a provisional summing up of Dibbets's ideas on photography, nature and abstraction; the conflict between visual and conceptual aspects has here been brought to a beautiful solution.

After the Comets a remarkable change in Dibbets's work set in. The horizon disappears, distant space makes way for phenomena from nearby reality. In the Structure Studies of water, grass, reeds and autumn leaves, as well as in the Color Studies of automobile fragments, the use of the camera is less striking than before, albeit in perfect accordance with the concept. The accent now lies more on the hidden structure within the motif itself or, as in the Color Studies, on the elusive world of reflecting color and light, than on the possibilities of the camera itself. In earlier works the photographs, in accordance with the concept of photography, have a fixed place in the totality of a sequence. But in the Structure Studies, for instance, we see how random closeups of the motif are mounted in rows or blocks. The coherence between the photographs now lies both in the way they are mounted and in the inherent structural affinity between parts of the motif. The question of whether a single photographic enlargement of the motif would not have sufficed directly brings to our attention the subtle articulation between the individual photographs. A continuous interplay of union and division, attraction and rejection, clashing and blending is to be seen along the almost invisible grid of intersections created by the montage of fragments. It is as if the intersections activate latent forces, thereby making a hidden structure in the motif visible. Each photograph is different and yet they are all the same, each photograph merely shows a random fragment of the chosen motif and yet matches all the other fragments. What these Structure Studies actually reveal are the rhythmical basic structures underlying the infinitely rich variety of nature.

In a group of subsequent works—Panoramas and Structure Studies of tiled floors, pavements and streets—the idea of the closeup structure is coupled with the ambiguity of the space that is perceived in an extreme form in Dibbets's Perspective Corrections. Once again, the motif is presented in closeups, this time, however, in the form of a sequence. The internal structure of the motif (the oblique lines of tiles and paving stones) is thus integrated into the external structure of the sequence. Each photograph in itself shows a fragment of a space in one-point perspective, but by the camera's rotation, visible in the sequence, the vanishing points shift and the obliqueness of the motif changes. As in the first Perspective Corrections, but in a much more complex way, the space that is thus created fascinates, not to say enthralls. On the one hand, the image, as in the Structure Studies of water and autumn leaves, is filled to the brim with nearby reality; on the other, the rotating perspective of the ground creates a moving, curving space that, like that of the Dutch Mountains, echoes the infinite curve of the earth's surface. While there is no horizon to be seen, proximity and infinity seem to interpenetrate fully.

The idea of infinity, suddenly so manifest in these panoramas of the ground on which we stand, unfolds before our eyes with the greatest complexity in the recent works inspired by architectural interiors. After due consideration, however, the idea can be seen to have been effective in Dibbets's photographic concept from the outset. As already suggested in the foregoing, it follows from the causal relationship between photography and reality that the photograph is by definition a fragment, a fragment without an identity of its own. In other words, each photograph implicitly raises questions about all the other possible fragments, and thus about everything that we do not see in the photograph. The photograph, however, cannot answer those questions because the rest of the world is hermetically sealed off by the viewfinder. Now in Dibbets's work we do see an answer, his answer, not implicitly, but explicitly. By virtue of the very acceptance of the photograph as a fragment and the seeking of a solution irrespective of the actual photograph, he succeeds each time anew in creating a structure that is self-contained and yet open-ended, a structure that reconciles the scale and size of an individual work with a concept, but that, like the open structure of a Mondrian, at the same time radiates to all sides and evokes a dimension of infinity.

In the context of this article there is room only for some brief comments on Dibbets's recent works, in which that aspect of infinity is elaborated in the most complex manner. The camera moves from the ground on which we stand upwards to ceilings and arches, cupolas and roofs, transforming the spaces in which man gives the most concrete form to his beliefs into true interiors. The most important element in our experience and perception of space is undoubtedly the awareness of *interior* versus *exterior,* of being inside or outside, regardless of whether we associate that interior with a primitive hut, a house or a cathedral. This awareness, being so universal, permeates our entire existence and is, in my opinion, the crux of Dibbets's works on the theme of architecture. Just as in his Panoramas the infinity of the ground on which we stand is reflected in what is close at hand, so the immense arch of the sky, under which man has built roofs since time began, is reflected in Dibbets's interpretations of finite interior spaces.

Once again we see how concepts that were more or less separately given form in Dibbets's early works are now integrated into a new, far-reaching concept. Light, perspectival ambiguity, camera angle and movement, proximity and distance, and structural relationships within a sequence of photographs unite to form a self-evident whole, here, as in earlier works, but more elaborately, in combination with more classical techniques such as drawing and watercolor painting. I have not yet mentioned the use of those more classical techniques. Drawing techniques are applied in Dibbets's work for diverse reasons, sometimes for the purpose of visualizing a concept more forcefully (*Horizontal Construction of a Sea 9°–81°*, 1973; p. 37), sometimes to strengthen the structure of a sequence (*Construction 330°*, 1979; p. 43), and in later works quite often to extend the photographic illusion into a drawn illusion beyond the confines of the photograph. In *Black and White Structure, No. 4* (1978; p. 110), for instance, the sequence of photographs showing paving stones blends at each end into a pencil drawing that becomes progressively fainter until it disappears completely. The visual structure of sequence and motif is thus transformed first into the more tactile structure of a drawing and subsequently into the elusive spatiality of the white paper. The same technique recurs in the works dealing with architecture in which the drawing is absorbed into a base of semi-transparent watercolor.

Dibbets's interpretation of the architectural interior offers an original view of experiences that are perhaps common to all of us, but which we have never seen *before* our eyes: the simultaneous experience of inside and outside. In the beautiful work entitled *Bourges I* (1981; p. 44), the structure of pillars, windows and vaulted ceilings extends outward into a drawing that mentally completes the space. Supported by this we translate the open circular shape of the sequence into a movement of our vision, in exactly the same way as when, standing in a cathedral, our eyes are drawn into the space extending above us. The difference is that here the sensation is given form on a two-dimensional plane. A one-point perspective painting, bound up as it is with a single viewpoint and a stable horizon, can never visualize such experiencing of interior spaces. The space that Dibbets creates, though, transcends the perspective of the individual photograph. His sequences curve around an "empty" center, expand from that center in all directions, blending into a drawing and eventually dissolving into the indeterminate space of the white paper or into the receding shades of a watercolor wash. This outward movement, this movement toward infinity, however, keeps turning back to the center in which it is anchored: the point where the human eye coincides with the eye of the camera.

Many years ago the French-American writer Julien Green, always a most careful observer, wrote the following lines about photographing people: "The problem is not to copy, but to create anew. Nothing is quite so motionless as a photograph album. It is useless to tell me that a photograph does not lie, that it is an indisputable likeness of life itself; I can see no more in a photograph than the reflection of an absent person."[8]

Dibbets will no doubt agree. He does not photograph people, and, remarkably enough, in the few works he has called self-portraits, all we see is the shadow cast by someone taking a photograph. This shadow in no way recalls the "reflection of an absent person." Quite the contrary, it brings to mind an invisible and yet mysteriously present individual who, in his alliance with the eye of the camera, observes, experiences and contemplates the world.

Translated by Ina Rike

Notes

1. Henri Cartier-Bresson, *The Decisive Moment* (New York: Simon and Schuster, 1952).

2. André Pieyre de Mandiargues and Ferdinando Scianna, *Henri Cartier-Bresson, Portraits* (London: William Collins Sons, 1984), p. 57.

3. André Pieyre de Mandiargues, *Henri Cartier-Bresson, Photoportraits* (New York: Thames and Hudson, 1985).

4. Yves Bonnefoy, *Henri Cartier-Bresson, Photographer* (Boston: New York Graphic Society, 1979), p. 5.

5. Roland Barthes, *La chambre claire* (Cahiers du Cinéma, Gallimard Seuil, 1980), pp. 54–56, 138.

6. André Bazin, *What is Cinema?* (Berkeley: University of California Press, vol. I, 1967).

7. Interview with Jan Dibbets, *Haagse Post,* vol. 67, no. 10, 8 March 1980, p. 94.

8. Julien Green, *Le Langage et son double/The Language and its Shadow* (Paris: Editions de la Difference, 1985), p. 238.

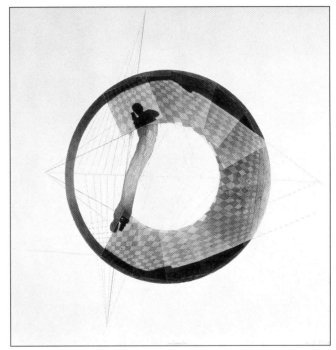

Spoleto Self-Portrait 1981
color photographs and pencil
on cardboard, two parts
28¾ x 28¾ each
73 x 73
Private collection

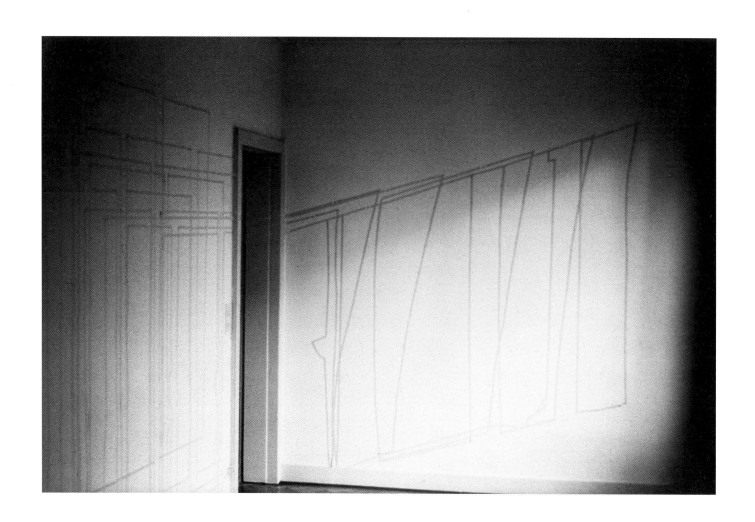

**Shadows Taped off on a
Wall, Museum Haus Lange,
Krefeld** 1969
documentary photographs
record this temporary
installation

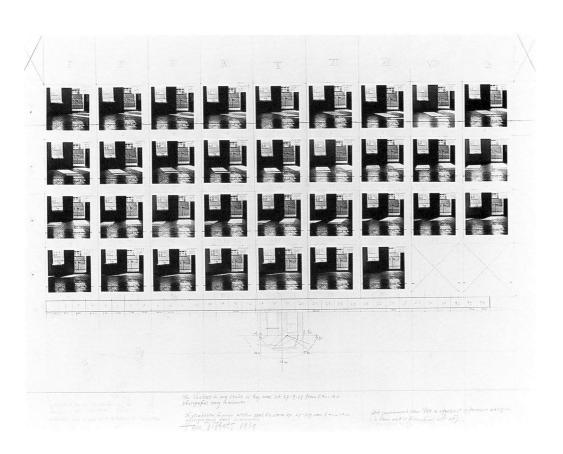

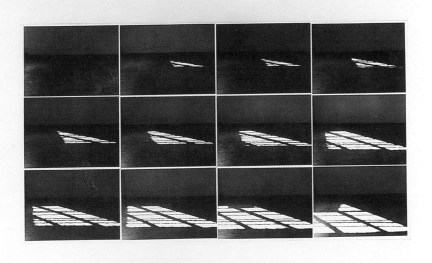

**The Shadows in My
Studio** 1969
black and white photographs
and pencil on paper
29½ x 39½
75 x 100
Collection Rolf Preisig

**Shadows on the Floor
of the Sperone Gallery**
1971
black and white photographs
on paper
27½ x 39½
70 x 100
Collection Panza di Biumo

**The Shortest Day at
the Van Abbemuseum**
1970
color photographs on board
70 x 67¼
177 x 171
Collection Stedelijk Van
Abbemuseum, Eindhoven

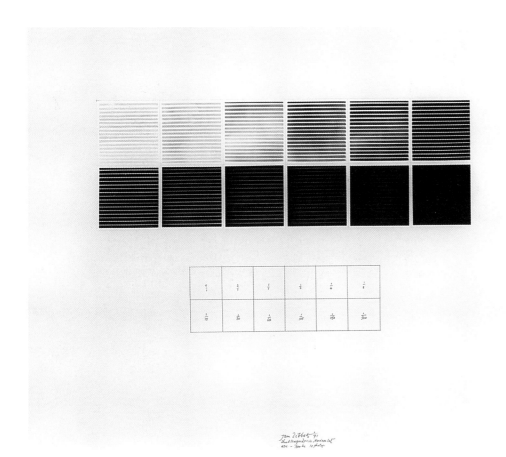

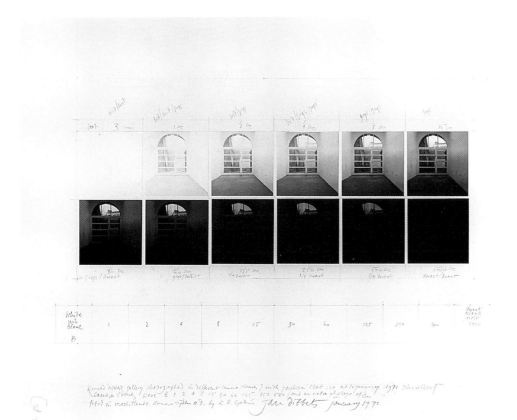

**Shutterspeed Piece,
Horizontal** 1971
black and white photographs
and pencil on paper
23½ x 29½
60 x 75
Collection Daled

**Shutterspeed Piece,
Konrad Fischer's
Gallery I** 1971
black and white photographs
and pencil on paper
23½ x 28¾
60 x 73
Private collection

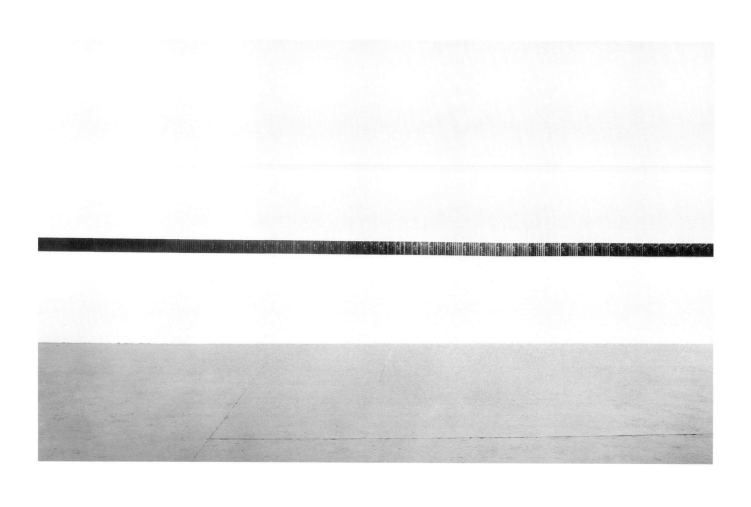

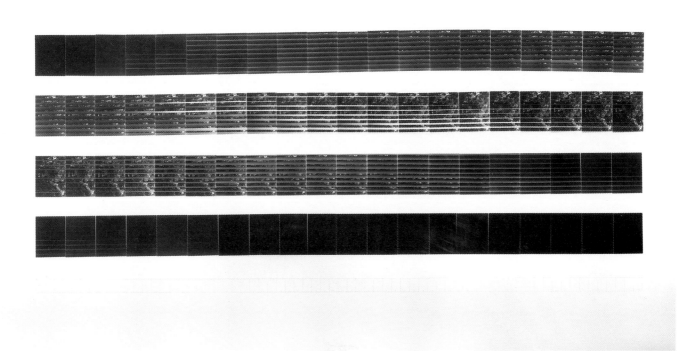

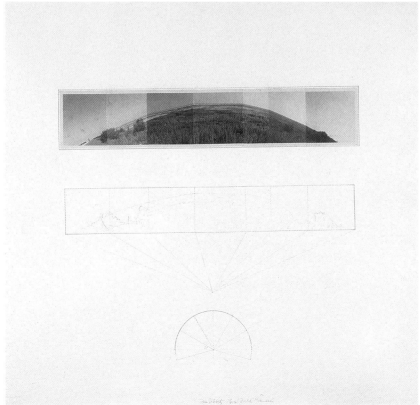

Study for Dutch Mountain/Sea 1971
color photographs, felt-tip pen
and pencil on paper
20 x 24½
51 x 62
Collection Ida Leach

Dutch Mountain, Land 1972
color photographs
and pencil on paper
27½ x 27½
70 x 70
Private collection

(opposite)
Louverdrape, Vertical
1971
color photographs
on aluminum
9½ x 657
24 x 1670
Private collection
(Installation view)

Louverdrape, Black to Black 1971–1972
color photographs and
pencil on paper
32 x 60¼
81 x 153.5
Private collection

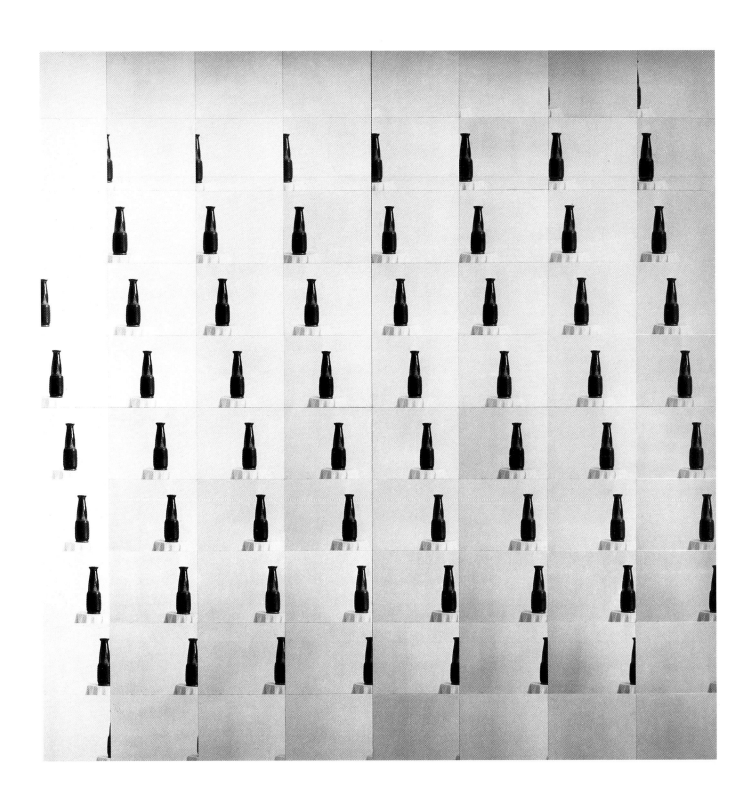

**Film: Painting Black Vase,
Horizontal** 1972
color photographs on
aluminum
75 x 75½
190 x 192
Collection Museum Ludwig,
Cologne

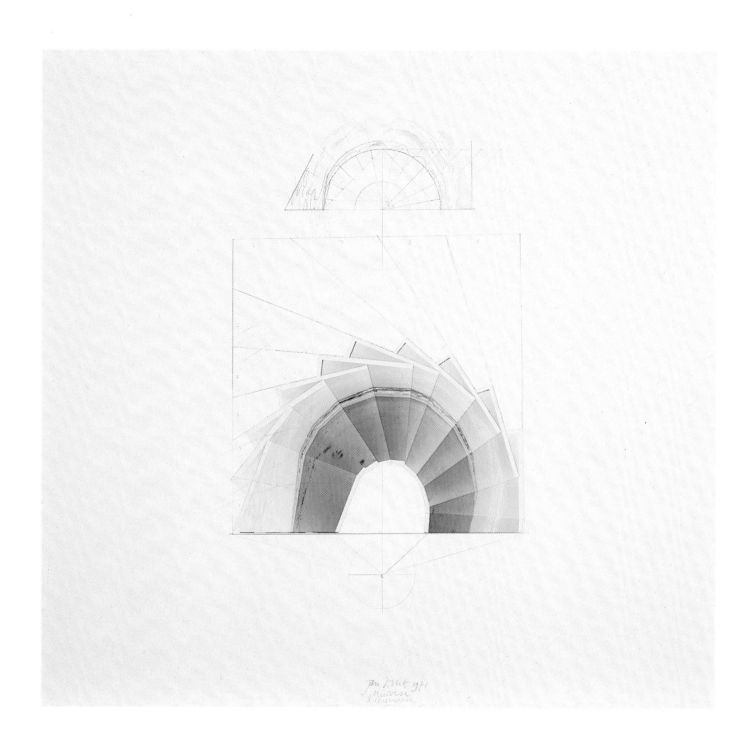

Universe/A Construction
1971
color photographs and
pencil on paper
25½ x 27½
65 x 70
Collection Stedelijk Museum,
Amsterdam

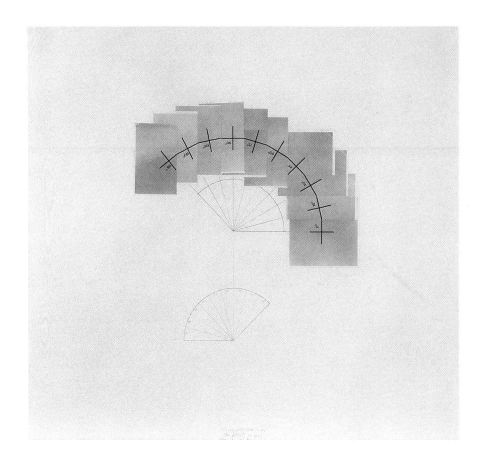

**Reconstruction Cross
0°–135°** 1972–1973
black and white photographs
and pencil on paper
20 x 22½
50 x 57
Private collection

**Reconstruction Sea
0°–135°** 1972–1973
black and white photographs
and pencil on paper
20 x 22¼
50 x 56.5
Private collection

(opposite)
**Horizontal Construction
of a Sea 9°–81°** 1973
color photographs
and pencil on paper
28¾ x 40
73 x 102
Collection Walther-Blume

Land 9°–81° 1973
nine individually framed
color photographs
7¾ x 49 gradually decreasing
to 7¾ x 1¼
19.5 x 124.5 gradually
decreasing to 19.5 x 3
Private collection
(Installation view)

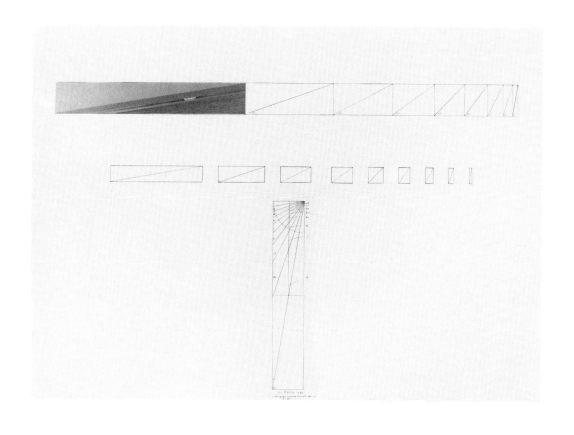

Big Comet 3°–60°,
Sky/Sea/Sky 1973
twenty individually framed
color photographs
177 x 236, installation
dimensions
450 x 600
Collection Stedelijk Museum,
Amsterdam

Waterstructure 1975
color photographs
and pencil on paper
28½ x 40
73 x 102
Collection Joan S. Sonnabend

Structure Study 1974
color photographs
and pencil on paper
20 x 25½
50 x 65
Private collection

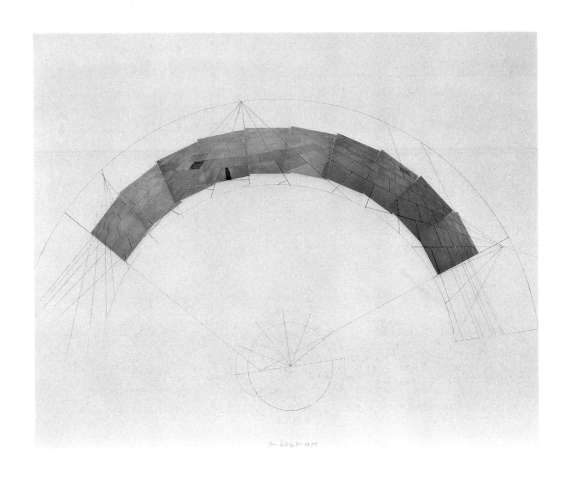

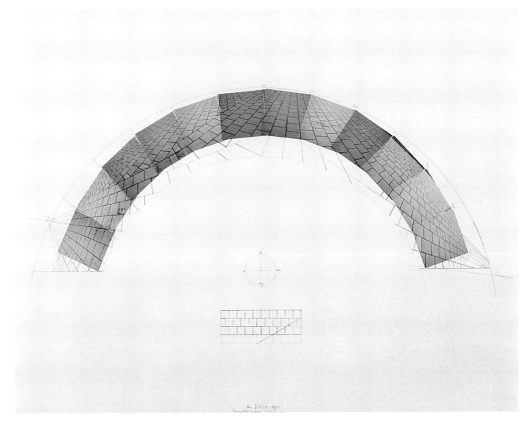

**Structure Panorama
Study** 1977
color photographs
and pencil on paper
20 x 25½
50 x 65
Private collection

**Structure Panorama
Study** 1977
color photographs
and pencil on paper
20 x 25½
50 x 65
Collection Joan S. Sonnabend

**Black and White
Structure** 1978
black and white photographs
and pencil on paper
31½ x 39½
80 x 100
Private collection

Colorstudy B1, 2, 3 1976
color photographs on paper
32½ x 32½ each of three
83 x 83
Private collection

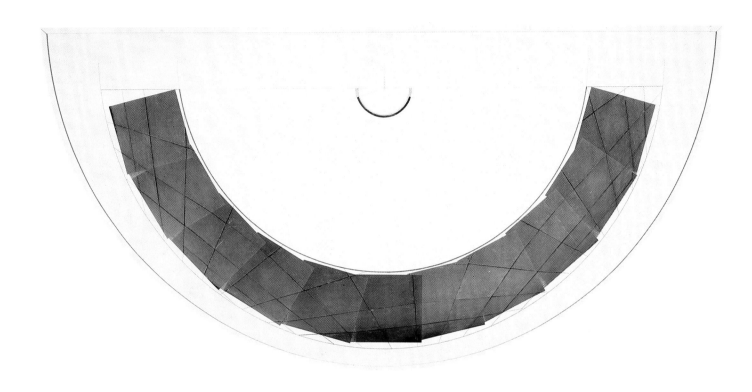

Construction 330° 1979
color photographs
and pencil on paper
mounted on chipboard
57¾ x 115
146.5 x 292.5
Collection Stedelijk Museum,
Amsterdam

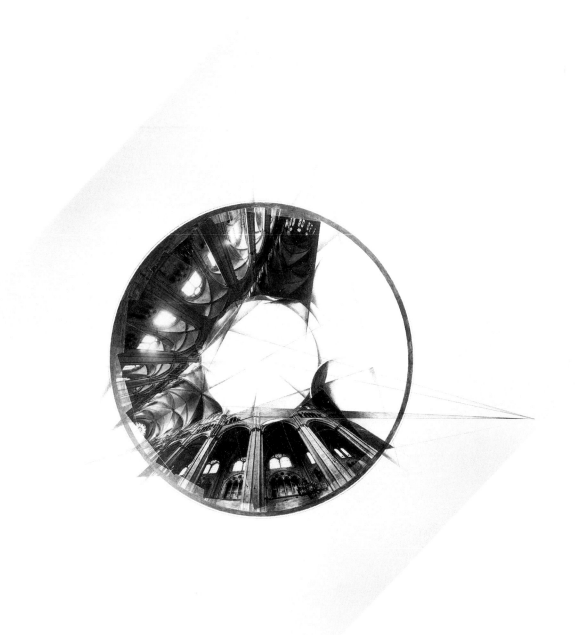

Bourges I 1981
color photographs
and pencil on paper
72¾ x 72¾
185 x 185
Collection Stedelijk Museum,
Amsterdam

Dublin Arcade II 1983
color photographs and
pencil on paper
28¾ × 40
73 × 102
Private collection

**Perspective Correction,
My Studio I, 1: Square on
Wall** 1969
black and white photograph
on photographic canvas
43¼ x 43¼
110 x 110
Collection Gian Enzo Sperone

The Eye Framed and Unframed

R.H. Fuchs

When Jan Dibbets was ten years old, his father took him to the Rijksmuseum in Amsterdam to see the national art treasures, an obligatory visit for all good Dutch boys, sweetened after by a boat trip around the city's canals. Dibbets remembers how his father explained Rembrandt's *Nightwatch,* telling him it was the greatest Dutch painting. It certainly was impressive to a small boy, but Jan preferred the cool, transparent church interiors of Pieter Janszoon Saenredam. His father, as a father should do, was introducing him to Dutch culture; he however started to look at paintings, at *individual* paintings, as an artist does. Eight years later when he went to art school, by then convinced that Piet Mondrian was the greatest painter of the twentieth century, he was shocked to learn that in art school, his view was not generally held, and he was taught to draw in the traditional manner, after casts of antique sculpture. The daily practice of learning the skills of art, the orientation toward craft, made him almost forget Mondrian. From the point of view of the crafts he was learning, other artists seemed more exciting, artists such as Francis Bacon, Max Beckmann, and Pablo Picasso, because they are, on the level of craft, more accessible and more useful than Mondrian. Beckmann or Picasso can teach you how to make an interesting painting; one can imitate them with slight variations. But to imitate Mondrian is ridiculous. Mondrian requires a different frame of mind. For Mondrian you must give up what you always thought was beautiful.

• •

One September afternoon in 1967, Dibbets cut a rough trapezoid in the thick turf of his sister's lawn. He then made a photograph from an optical angle that made the original shape appear to be a rectangle, lifting itself from the ground and aligning itself, flat and parallel, to the picture plane. The published version of this first Perspective Correction is a dry diagrammatic drawing of how the illusion was constructed, carrying the original small photograph only as a visual footnote. This conceptual form of presentation may have taken something away from the fresh beauty of the idea. But Dibbets was a young artist, fresh out of school, just finding his voice.

As a form, the Perspective Corrections reflected the aesthetic concerns of the period—the taste for simple structures and undramatic, almost documentary forms of presentation. Many young artists were looking for new ways to make art, or for new aspects of traditional forms to develop. The problem for a young artist in a context of competitive experimentation is not so much to hit on a super-new trick but, and this Dibbets knew from the beginning, to develop a basic line or form capable of sustaining expansion and variation over time.

In 1966–1967, Dibbets was making objects constructed upon shifts between two forms (one real, one suggested) or between two materials. He began with paintings, or rather pictorial objects. Small canvases, painted a monochrome pink and pale blue (colors that made them lose material weight), were stacked upon each other to form a sculpture or painting; or, rectangular canvases were laid out on the floor to form another shape, for example, a lozenge made of rectangles. The essence of these works, in a structural sense, was that with equal elements of one particular shape one could construct other shapes. Though perhaps not spectacular, this discovery provided an orientation previously lacking in Dibbets's work. At art school he had made paintings, but each painting had not suggested the next one. In making a construction with small canvases he had found a structural element, tentative, but consistent in itself.

In the same period he made other objects: a table with a grass top; a bunch of dead tree branches, including among them one artificial branch of blue neon; and two conic forms whose points are connected by a thin line of neon, one form borrowing from the other. These objects were experimental. They proposed a direction, but no precise form. Yet Dibbets realized that these were no longer isolated paintings. They sprang from coherent drifts of thought and intuition.

He spent the first part of 1967 in London where he had a scholarship for St. Martin's School of Art. Contacts with other young artists there, such as Barry Flanagan and Richard Long, enforced his instinctual working method. He started to work directly on the ground. He cut out a square of lawn and from one corner rolled up a strip of turf halfway toward the center. A square produced a cylinder. Or, repeating a principle previously used in the constructed paintings, he cut a square of turf in a lawn and subdivided that square into four equal smaller squares. He placed two squares on top of two others. Looked at from a certain angle, the square becomes a lozenge, and the work a construction of lozenges of optically different sizes.

Although Dibbets came to photography almost by chance, he quickly realized the powerful subtlety of the medium. When photographing one form he observed how that shape could optically metamorphose into another. And photographing his grass works gave him the idea for the Perspective Corrections in which a change of viewpoint resulted in an optical change of shape. The earlier accidental forms (dependent on the movement of the viewer) became inescapably fixed in the still photograph. Instead of leaving the optical transformation of shape to chance, Dibbets now chose to make that transformation less gradual and more arresting and, as a visual experience, more abstract. In fact, he reversed the previous method, making a formal construction and controlling what would be seen by the viewer.

The first Perspective Corrections transformed his work from experimental and spontaneous to controlled and analytical. After deciding the type of shape or construction that should appear in a photograph, or rather *on the surface* of a photograph, Dibbets then designed the formal setup needed to produce that shape, thus making not a photograph but a photographic construction. What one sees on the photograph is, in the optical sense, not what has been photographed: an illusion becomes an abstraction; or an illusionistic form is abstracted into a different shape. The illusion is cancelled out by the appearance of the abstract shape.

The method and technique of the Perspective Corrections are extremely simple, but at the same time they are complete, as complete and beautiful as a clear circle. The series gave Dibbets a whole range of formal and aesthetic possibilities; it also cleared up the relationship of his work to older art as well as to the art of his contemporaries. The constructed paintings, the grass "sculptures" or the ambiguous objects moved in the aesthetic context of optical abstract art, touching on Minimalism, then emerging. As a practical use of an aesthetic those works are adequate but they are also ambivalent. The Perspective Corrections began while he was making other optical abstractions. The first one dates from September 1967 but the two cones with the neon line between them was made in early 1968. His experiments were overlapping. Of course those diverse experiments were coherent in their structural premise (shifts between forms and materials) but they still produced highly diverse images—images with quite divergent potential for development. Somehow Dibbets decided that the *type* of image in the Perspective Corrections (not, I must emphasize, their construction) was more important to him than the image of the more objectlike work. That is to say, in the still image of the Perspective Corrections (a shape going through a sudden but invisible transformation and then coming to rest) Dibbets's memory of Mondrian, and even of Saenredam, came alive again. He came back to what he had always felt art should be. That dream had been interrupted by other "inventions" at a time when he was not yet able to make the perfect choice.

The rediscovery of Mondrian, and a more active understanding of his paintings, pointed the way and made Dibbets realize that the objectlike works, when pursued as a form, might in the end become too bizarre or too maverick. To go on with them would mean to move quickly from invention to invention. That was their character, they wanted to be surprising. But Dibbets (we now know, twenty years later) prefers to think and formulate in long lines that are sometimes parallel, then cross over, and then perhaps are parallel again. That is how his oeuvre developed—controlled and unhurried.

The theme of the Perspective Corrections proved to be effective and fruitful. Between September 1967 and late 1969 Dibbets made about forty versions. Some of them brought him close to what he admired most in the paintings of the late Mondrian: flexibility of shape in a composition as clear and firm as a window. The series was carried through in a methodical manner. Most of these works were made on grass, using white rope to lay out the forms in horizontal, vertical or diagonal lines, rectangular or diagonal crosses, and in circles. A large number of them existed in two forms: as a drawing or description of the construction, with small photographs almost as illustrations, and as enlarged photographic transfers on canvas. In the large, purely visual versions, the resulting image is dissociated from its construction. The step of enlarging the image and eliminating the construction may now seem almost insignificant. At the time, however, it was a major step, not at all easy to take, toward an image that would be independently visual as opposed to an image that is the translation of a conceptual construction.

At issue: does art need a palpable expression, or can it be completely conceptual? Dibbets wanted to take a clear position. He did not want to be a photographer of clever optical tricks, he had somehow to separate the image as the visual result of a technical process from the technique itself. The drawings—the constructions formulated on paper—could show their "photographic" origin because that is what drawings traditionally do. They show the outline of an image, its skeleton form. But after the drawing, the "full" work completes and, in a sense, supersedes the drawing. It took a while, however, to come to grips with the problem of enlargement. For instance, in some of the large works, especially those with ropes on grass, the material distinction between the two elements tends to become heavy through too much articulation. The grass, which in the small size photographs on the drawings, appears as an even gray, in the large version becomes highly accented and thus a bit heavy; and the rope is not quite just a white line. Probably the last versions are therefore the most successful, made not on a lawn but in the interior of Dibbets's studio. The best of these is a square on the wall of the studio. It is a small square penciled on a white wall, so light that it seems to float. The square on the studio wall is mysterious, abstract to the point that the photographic aspect is completely forgotten. It is, in a way, miraculous.

In constructing the Perspective Corrections something happened to the spatial structure of the resulting image. In the photograph, the geometrical form laid out on the lawn or drawn on the wall changed into a different shape on the *surface* of the photographic image. The ground supporting the original shape was carried along, it seems, in the process of visual transformation and became frontal too, like the "corrected" shape. The illusionistic space, which is the natural space of photography, is thus eliminated: it is as if space is being pushed forward, almost out of the image. This happens especially in the Perspective Corrections on grass, when the white lines of rope touch the edge of the picture itself and when the first and second images overlap. The later works, in the studio, leave an illusionistic photographic space intact, which is then confronted with the "corrected" shape coming forward to the picture's ambiguous surface (defined by the small transparent square) and the illusionistic "interior" of the photograph.

In this type of picture, in which the abstract form, flat on the surface, merges with the unavoidable illusionism of photography, Dibbets's work, for the first time, comes close to certain qualities in Mondrian's painting. For Dibbets articulates his work within a network of other art. He is a contemporary artist inventing new visual forms and expressions, but at the same time he is aware of the fact that he is also continuing great traditions in Western art. When, in the Perspective Corrections, he brings a form to the surface of the picture plane, making abstract what was illusionistic, he quite consciously brings to a conclusion a long line of development in Western painting, most clearly in still-life painting. Compare, for instance, a seventeenth-century Dutch still life with a still life by Cézanne, and then continue that comparison up to Mondrian. The seventeenth-century still life presents a corner of a table with objects on it in illusionistic and, more importantly, atmospheric space. In such a picture, the light (coming from an outside source) articulates various objects (a glass, a fish, fruit, bread, lemon, and so on) by touching their surfaces, making colors, textures and shapes visible—but more significantly, making visible the *differences* in colors, textures and shapes.

In these early paintings, one sees a symphony of objects in light and shade, and because the light is always soft and gentle, the image is always intimate. It is hidden, discreetly curled up in the interior space of the picture almost like a pearl in its shell. As the objects in a seventeenth-century still life are hardly ever parallel with the picture plane, they detach themselves from the picture's surface. A Cézanne still life is more frontal. He emphasizes, in the position of the objects, the actual rectangle of the picture: most lines (or directions) run parallel to the horizontal and vertical edges of the picture. The composition, therefore, tends to move forward toward the surface of the painting. This effect is heightened by the way the paint is applied. Contrary to the seventeenth-century picture, in Cézanne there is almost no attention to texture because there is no independent light that reflects differently on a shining glass than on the dull surface of a piece of bread. In a Cézanne painting a lemon is an oval yellow shape, and an apple is a slightly flattened red shape. Visually they have the same impact. They are equal because they do not have the texture of their species, rather, they have the texture of paint.

This "system" of stabilizing a composition of shapes upon the surface of a painting, within the concrete boundaries of its rectangular edge, was carried further by Mondrian to the point where he made the image spatially more ambiguous. Because Mondrian used, as visual elements, simple rectangular shapes and strongly contrasting colors within grids of black lines on white grounds, his pictures are extremely transparent. The different shapes and colors suggest various positions in an abstract space whose "parameters" are defined by the white of the ground and the black of the lines. The surface of a Mondrian painting does not close, it is transparent; the surface of a Cézanne still life, on the other hand, is dense with paint. Thus, on the surface, a Mondrian picture is absolutely stable, even static— but spatially it is tense and nervous. It was, I believe, this quality in Mondrian that Dibbets had in mind, as an artistic point of reference, when he began the Perspective Corrections. In the interior versions, most of all, he was able to shape the tension between frontal surface and spatial depth, because photography enabled him to make the spatial background seem to be more real.

We see a realistic photograph of Dibbets's studio, complete with floor, wall and windows; and in that interior a square appears on the surface of the image that, it seems, should not be there. The "corrected" shape, which gives focus to the image, is real as surface, whereas the background interior is paradoxically real as illusion. In the Perspective Corrections photography is used in a very simple way, almost as a record of the moment in which the eye, in the right position, would see the transformation. But the photograph intensifies that moment, gives it greater urgency. It effectively eliminates perceptual digression, cutting out the visual surroundings. Unlike the eye, which is never completely at rest, the photograph does not move. Thus the photographic Perspective Correction is also a perceptual fragment, and as such it is used as an element in the construction and reconstruction of perceptual processes.

It was in this general direction that Dibbets, after the Perspective Corrections, continued his work. He started to use single photographs, for instance, as documentary moments, moments of acute perception, in order to reconstruct a certain process in time. In these works photography was used to give a rhythm to time, or to make time stand still. In 1969 Dibbets made a work called *The Shadows in My Studio* (p. 29), for which he set up the camera in a fixed position in front of a window and the open door of his studio. Then from 8:40 am to 2:10 pm he took a photograph every ten minutes, documenting the movement of light and shadow on the studio floor, how they moved with the sun, describing the day. The work, thirty-four photographs mounted on white board, is a linear condensation of time. It makes time visible as moving light. It gives form, or rather imposes a rhythmical form of equal repetitive movements, to a process that would otherwise never be visible with such a degree of concentration. There are several versions of this work made in different locations—as there are several versions of a related work *The Shortest Day at the Van Abbemuseum* (1970; p. 30). For the latter, he set up the camera in front of a window in order to photograph the movement of daylight every ten minutes from dawn to sunset, producing a portrait of a day in terms of light. In other constructions, done one year later in 1971, he used a related but more abstract idea. One could say that the Sunrise-Sunset or the Shadow Pieces are documentary and naturalistic. They use real time (up to an entire day), then come to a concentrated image (or visual record) of that real time.

In 1971 Dibbets used the mechanical properties of the camera, systemic photographic time, to change the amount of light. In the so-called Shutterspeed Pieces he photographed a half-closed venetian blind twelve times, each time cutting the shutterspeed by half, from four seconds, producing an almost white photograph, to 1/500 second, producing a black photograph. I have the impression, however, that these works, using the time controlling mechanism of the camera itself, were an intermezzo, because they paradoxically were too abstract: they were pure constructions, lacking the ambiguity of other work in which there is a contrast between real and photographic time.

The Shortest Day at the Van Abbemuseum was first made as a slide projection. The eighty slides, taken at ten minute intervals covering the entire day, were to be projected at ten second intervals upon the wall opposite the window through which they were originally taken. Thus the work, which is a formalized structure recording the progression of real time, visible as the light of dawn and the fading evening light, was to be seen by the viewer in equivalent real time. The work was presented as process.

At the time Dibbets was interested in the structure itself, in the structural realization rather than the form of presentation. He had enlarged Perspective Corrections, transferring them onto canvases as though they were paintings. These remained enlargements; the image itself did not change, although it changed in visual impact. A series of small photographs, recording the shadows in his studio, were mounted in horizontal lines on paper, to be read like words on a page. But what was Dibbets's essential idea? Around 1970, his work became structurally and physically more complex, and the definition of what these works were, how they should behave visually, became more and more problematic. The Perspective Corrections, up to 1969, and later works surveying interior space (such as Numbers on a Wall) and works measuring and reconstructing geographical distances, using photographs as points of reference, were all characterized by the particular analytic approach to visual phenomena that was the framework of Conceptual Art.

Conceptual Art was a specific development and transformation of Minimal Art. When Frank Stella made his Black Stripe paintings he gave them an image that precisely articulated the shape and surface of the paintings themselves. He did not create, as previous artists had done, an image that separated itself from the rectangular shape of the painting. After that, conceptual artists avoided that modernist pictorial problem (which Cézanne and Mondrian and others had begun to recognize); they concentrated instead on internal structure and the rules of image making, or more generally on transferring visual and linguistic content. They soon found other means to present their work: language, photography, diagrammatic drawing. Thus, it can be shown that the visual "strategies" Jan Dibbets used for his first photographic work ultimately derive from the context of Conceptual Art. Initially they were borrowed techniques (or techniques simply present in the practice of the period). As a discipline these methods gave his early work strong formal support. At the same time, because of his background and traditions, Dibbets's instincts drew him to an image with a more pictorial quality.

In the dry, diagrammatic character of the first Perspective Corrections Dibbets had not found his mature artistic nature, and he soon started to enlarge the images to see whether these autonomous constructions would hold up without a constructionist "explanation." The enlarged photographic constructions made around 1970 convinced him that a work could be conceptually acceptable and at the same time have a strong image. And what is more, the single photograph was, in terms of the construction to which it belonged, an abstract, flexible element, and simultaneously a naturalistic fragment. He sensed that the paradoxical relationship between abstract form and structure and naturalistic fragment presented a wide and exciting range of possibilities for construction of wonderful and intriguing images. Because of that strange, ambiguous opposition, these images would still be acceptable within the contemporary, conceptualist aesthetic. Dibbets also decided that there was no reason why his photography should not be in color.

In *The Shortest Day at the Van Abbemuseum,* his first work in color, Dibbets decided to mount the photographs in horizontal rows on a single panel, as he had done in other instances, because he was fully aware that the development of his work would run into trouble if it did not take into account the visual power and beauty of the single image. Therefore, the earlier projection was dismantled and the eighty photographs were mounted on a panel, thus creating a much stronger work. The change of color, for instance, bluish light in the morning going toward red in the afternoon, was invisible in the projection as the intervals between the slides were rather long. On the panel the work is more concentrated; it has the compressed perceptual form that has become a major characteristic of Dibbets's art. In such works, his art is about perception itself; and in his hands the photograph is the logical means with which to articulate forms and modes of perception. *The Shortest Day at the Van Abbemuseum* is an extended perception of light transformed and compressed into a perception of a completely different duration. But the measured structure of that perception remains intact. Its serial and analytic character are articulated more forcefully in the photographic panel, which is synthetic, than in the projection which is, in the end, too naturalistic in its imitation of time. This work shapes perception, making it an autonomous, concrete object of artistic research, just as Frank Stella's structure of stripes shapes a painting. The shape of perception gives Dibbets's work its singular form.

The Sunrise-Sunset Pieces reconstruct a precise duration of time in equal photographic moments. Reading a line of photographs, one can reconstruct a day. In 1970 Dibbets applied the same principle to the photographic reconstruction of space. These works, titled Numbers on a Wall, are few, but they were seminal, because in the end they led to the first panoramic pieces and thus to the most significant structural principle in Dibbets's work. The Numbers on a Wall Pieces were made by setting up the camera at a distance of roughly two meters from a wall in the gallery in which the piece was made. On the wall the artist drew two vertical lines defining, left and right, the expanse of wall that was visible in the camera's viewfinder. Centered between the two lines he put the number 1. He took the photograph, then moved the camera to the right, keeping the same distance from the wall (in order not to destroy the unity of scale) until the right line of the first photograph became the left edge of the second photograph. At the right edge of the new area seen through the viewfinder, he drew a new line; between the lines he placed the number 2. In that precise, methodical way he photographed all four walls of the room and then mounted the photographs in sequence around the periphery of the gallery. The concept of these works—to make visible in a single constructed image a space that the human eye cannot take in without moving around—was fascinating and effective. Also, the experiment helped to define and clarify other questions about the use of photography. Dibbets found that photographic space is more complex to handle than photographic time, which in the end is always a momentary fragment of real time. Photographic space is a synthetic of something else: real space.

These first works about space were simple and direct, but possibly too close to architectural documentation. Dibbets then decided to vary his approach in a panoramic survey of his studio, setting up the camera on a fixed point and turning it around 360 degrees horizontally, photographing walls, doors, windows, moving 30 degrees for each photograph. He then put the photographs together, maintaining their visual continuity and producing a curving line. On paper the complete panorama became strangely fragmentary, visually completely different from the rectangular shape of the actual room.

These works introduced the notion of the unexpected into Dibbets's work, the difference between the method and its calculated result. In his recent constructions the final shape that the photograph will take is largely unknown. Experience has given Dibbets a sense of what is to come, but the surprise at the end is more important than the calculation of it. That surprise occurred for the first time in *Panorama, My Studio* (1971; p. 82).

Previously the result had been almost completely known beforehand; the Perspective Corrections were based on total visual control, starting with a geometric shape on the floor or wall, designed to become another shape by way of precisely placed photographic interventions. From that work one could draw a direct line to the 1977 Panoramas and to the more complex Saenredam Constructions.

One wonders hypothetically why Dibbets did not move ahead with greater speed in 1971. To move ahead the artist must be able to see ahead. The irregular shape of *Panorama, My Studio* was a surprise, and possibly not quite what he wanted at that time. In 1971, Dibbets was still testing photography as a means to achieve complete confidence and control. Typical of his quiet, unhurried way was the decision to ignore the surprise for the time being, and to employ other methods to construct a panorama.

Thus, after *Panorama, My Studio* he applied the same formal principle, fixing the camera's view on the horizon of a park landscape and of the sea. But this time he mounted the photographs in a straight, horizontal line. These images seem to be undulating: you see the trees, or the sea, coming toward you and then receding. They are images of deep, illusionistic space, yet also undeniably flat, as they are constructions of equal, flat elements. At the same time he worked on a film loop about the horizon of the sea. By moving the camera up and down, the image showed the horizon as a line moving up and down. Sometimes the sea would fill the screen completely, sometimes there would only be sky; most of the time, however, sea and sky would be visible together, introducing an illusionistic sense of space.

In another film loop he tilted the camera forty-five degrees; consequently, the horizon moved diagonally across the screen. The project (conceived for the 1972 Venice Biennale) was designed to have two or three adjacent screens, with projectors moving at different speeds, in order to create a complex spectacle. Yet in this work too, the shape and movement of the images are strictly controlled. As in the early Panoramas, and in the Perspective Corrections, natural perception is molded into a specific, unavoidable form. In this way the artist controls the eye of the viewer who knows that what he sees is not real. Some of these images went beyond normal, natural vision. Movement and different positions of the camera constructed forms that could exist as logical abstract constructions, or as photographic images, but not in real vision.

Natural perception is continuous and not governed by abstract external rules but by what is happening in front of one's eyes. Reacting to visual incidents and movement we follow the sequence of those incidents—changes of pattern, color, and so on—and we linger, concentrate, pass over. In itself, human vision is without predefined form. Photography usually does not interfere with this. In general, a photographer selects moments from a natural perceptual sequence because he considers them significant. Such photographs do not interrupt the sequence itself. Dibbets's use of photography is abstract (or rather, non-realistic) because it does interrupt the usual process of perception by imposing precise forms. He does not select an image from an existing sequence. The image he makes has not been seen before. It exists only as image and has no model in the real world.

In Dibbets's series of panoramic works called Dutch Mountains, he changed the position of the camera in relation to the horizon. In the earlier Panoramas the horizon remained the straight horizontal line we expect it to be. For the Dutch Mountains he set up the camera in such a way that, while completing a circle (or a part of a circle) it also moved up and down. Consequently, when the photographs were mounted in line, the horizon was curved instead of straight. The resulting image is supremely ambiguous because the abstract construction used photographs of a real landscape in color, making the image much more than a skeleton construction—making it, however unreal, look like the reconstruction of real nature.

But there is another more intimate way of reading Jan Dibbets's art. One can describe in objective terms the various forms and constructions he has used over the years. They are simple, clear forms that, in the course of their development, establish their own clarity. The achievement of this clarity—probably their final aesthetic goal—depends on an extremely subtle balance between the elements that make up an image. It cannot be established by method. In Dibbets's work method is only a basis for the order or logic of the construction. The final decisions are in the artist's eye. The logic of a construction may be perfect, but there remains the question of whether an image is right, whether its color is appropriate, whether it is too heavy, whether there is a sense of air and light. When an artist judges an image he has made, that image enters the artist's memory along with other art he has seen that echoes in his mind and makes up his personal awareness of quality in art. The sense of quality that largely determines the course of an oeuvre is like a continuous interior monologue, accepting and rejecting, or like a subterranean reservoir giving fertility to the soil above it. That sense of quality is accumulative and selective at the same time. It is not just historical knowledge of art. It is not that Mondrian made certain paintings that the artist must avoid because they exist already, but that Mondrian and other artists have demonstrated certain properties and qualities in their work that the living artist cannot forget. They are compelling—not like obstacles that bar every passage, but like beacons inviting the artist to go on.

These memories are often fragmentary, often incidental. They are not always logical or obvious. For example, I believe that Dibbets is impressed by Mondrian for a number of reasons. One of them surely is the extreme fragility of Mondrian's works as formal constructions, an aspect that perhaps only artists appreciate, because it is a quality not of theory but of craft. In this Mondrian differs profoundly from his contemporaries, Kasimir Malevich and Kurt Schwitters. The latter artists had something *within the picture,* a sort of hold, which gave real substance to their compositions. Malevich came from the tradition of icon painting that is non-illusionistic. The icon offers a sacred image fixed upon a flat ground of gold. Malevich too created a flat ground. His surface is thick as wood, and on that dense strong surface he constructed abstract compositions that came to rest upon that surface. The forms are stable because the surface is stable. Schwitters, being a Gothic artist by inspiration, worked with a system of accumulation. He accumulated fragments, letting them overlap and stacking them, until the work became dense and heavy, in a sense constructed, like architecture. But Mondrian had to design his transparent compositions within the airy, illusionistic space characteristic of the Dutch pictorial tradition. The black lines and the colored rectangles hang there, without anchor or weight, trembling like leaves in the breeze, in the silvery, atmospheric space of Van Goyen or Ruisdael.

That is the quality Dibbets has in mind when he thinks of Mondrian. When he remembers a painting by Piero della Francesca or Cézanne, it is not a heavy figure standing firmly on the ground, or two apples heavy in a bowl he thinks of, but something else: the slight suggestion of imbalance between the figures, the wavering of space, that almost unnoticeable irregularity of structure that introduces pictorial tension. It is impossible for a Dutch artist to establish a completely static form or a form that is completely at rest within its own compositional context. That makes Dibbets profoundly different from the contemporaries he admires most, from Sol LeWitt and Carl Andre whose forms have an inherent stillness, to Robert Ryman who creates a certain stability on the surface of his rather "nervous" paintings, so that within the confines of their surfaces, his works begin and end like completed melodies. Almost all of Dibbets's work, however, involves *states* of shapes between other shapes. The images are inherently mobile and changing.

The Perspective Corrections depict a shape that, by way of transformation, forms another shape. Tension exists because the second shape can, at any moment, fall back into the first shape. Similarly, the

Dutch Mountains are literally constructions organized by the mobile camera. They are works based on a formal intervention (the still photograph), moving into a state of motion (the moving camera). Just as in the paintings of Mondrian, the configuration of forms seems to be as changeable as the clouds in the Dutch sky.

The Dutch Mountains have an intriguing melodious quality, a movement that is like music. They suggest a specific length of time of perception that is different from the time of perception in other works. The Perspective Corrections, for instance, are almost instantaneous transformations, quick and abrupt. The Shutterspeed works have an even, measured quality, but they do not move as beautifully as the Dutch Mountains. The dancelike movement of some of the Dutch Mountains (some are slow, others quick, some seem to jump) can be judged when they are compared with works such as *0°–135° Horizontal* (1972; p. 96), which shows, in a highly abstracted, almost theoretical form, the essential principle of camera movement that is used more freely in the Dutch Mountains. For this work Dibbets drew a horizontal line on the wall and then photographed it ten times, moving the camera in a frontal, circular way, fifteen degrees for each shot. In the photographs, the line seems to move. The movement is crisp, precise, rhythmically dry.

The true subject of Dibbets's art is the shaping of modes of perception, and part of the shape is speed. Differences in speed are decisive elements in the way one sees and experiences Dibbets's work, and are consciously employed factors in making works. In the period in which he made the Dutch Mountains he also produced a series of pieces showing vases. For example, he put a small black vase on a table. He photographed this arrangement with a movie camera, in a slow horizontal pan (in other versions a vertical pan), starting and ending on white. In between, the vase appears and disappears, slowly and fractionally.

The film was then printed on photographic paper and mounted on a panel. To me, this exquisite still life is, in feeling and visual intention, the abstract opposite of the Dutch Mountains. The appearance and disappearance of the vase is so unbearably slow (much slower than the movement from image to image in *The Shortest Day at the Van Abbemuseum,* to which it is structurally related) that the vase seems not to move at all. The work is the image of stillness, yet the vase moves, moved by the slow camera. And then one year later, in a complete swing of the pendulum, he constructed (following and refining the precise principle of works like *0°–135° Horizontal*) a series of Comets that are images of absolute swiftness, the sea surging upwards.

The brilliant Comet series concluded, for the time being, Dibbets's preoccupation with beautiful, fantastically curving and leaping images of land and sea. The structural principle of these works had run its course, from the quiet early Panoramas to the dynamically constructed Comets. Instead of using the sharp line of the horizontal between land or sea and the sky that gave those works a strong formal backbone, he began to turn his attention to the texture of surfaces, and eventually to color.

Sometimes, in the course of his work, an artist risks a fundamental change, or at least a change that takes him far away from what he has been doing. Maybe this is simply a sense of adventure, for we expect occasional surprises from artists. But there are other, more serious motives for change; an artist changes course when the work threatens to go astray, or when it starts drifting on the flow of its own beauty. Jan Dibbets is very sensitive to that danger because his work, like the work of all good artists in the abstract-geometrical tradition, is formally extremely fragile. Works such as the Dutch Mountains balance, especially in their formal construction, on the edge. They can easily become self-indulgent; the images are beautiful and mysterious, sometimes dangerously elegant. When they pass that thin line beyond which formal control is lost, they fail.

Before that happens, the artist moves away to another, completely different area, to gain another point of view from which to look back on previous production with fresh eyes. Formal change thus becomes an important element in the judgment of one's own work, a critical activity an artist cannot do without, and therefore also an element in the development of the work, in choosing new themes and new formal strategies. A change of focus is not random or speculative, but a step consciously taken within the context of an artist's work. Work evolves along a central line and around certain central ideas that are sacred to the artist, in which he hears his own voice. Sometimes a group of works moves too far from those fundamental convictions, and then it is time to change.

I want to return, for a moment, to one of the last of the Perspective Corrections, *My Studio I, 1: Square on Wall* (1969; p. 46), and also to *Panorama, My Studio.* At some point in his early career an artist makes a work that touches the core of his sensibility. Though not always the best of his works (although *My Studio I, 1: Square on Wall* is one of the best), it may be (like *Panorama, My Studio*) less refined than later versions in the same vein, but these works are very honest; they are a self-discovery, an idea the artist wishes to cherish and defend. They are points of no return, and at the same time they indicate and open the way ahead.

In my view, the central line of Dibbets's art lies between those two works, or rather between the formal and aesthetic arguments they represent. The Perspective Correction is an image that comes forward and then, in one swift transformation, settles on the surface. It holds the surface and provides an almost stable focus of vision (not quite stable because it is off-center). *Panorama, My Studio* is a mobile image; scanning space, it has no center; it moves with its irregular form falling away to the right. Between these two kinds of imagery, Jan Dibbets's general idea of how an image should behave moves to and fro. From that point of view, which is critical because it represents a standard, one can see that the Comet Pieces are the ultimate form of the movable image.

Even if all the single elements of the Comet Pieces are strictly formal (diagonal divisions of sea and sky), their construction gives them an accelerating movement; from a firm base touching the floor they curve upwards to the point where the image literally disappears.

Beyond the disappearing image, there is nothing more. Thus Dibbets turned his attention to images that are almost motionless. In 1972, in Italy, he took the first photographs of the surface of water. He continued this more methodically in 1974 and 1975, adding works about the non-reflective structure of grass and leaves on the ground. The form of perception in these works is crystal clear. In the previous pieces, from Dutch Mountains to the Comets, perception was precisely shaped and framed for the beholder. The Structure works of water or leaves are pure surface. They bring the eye close to the surface that is very alive. In my view they are somewhat related, in their curious stillness, to the descriptions of interior space in the works called Numbers on a Wall. But the segments of wall that make up the construction of those works are boundaries, they define space; in the Structure Pieces, the surface is just surface.

The Structure Pieces are rectangular constructions using a number of photographs of the same general surface, but each of the photographic elements is slightly different. The surface we see is therefore unified, as water or leaves, but also differentiated. Because of these slight differences, from element to element, the surface never really comes to rest. It keeps vibrating and therefore does not completely identify with the surface of the photographic image itself. The works look straightforward but in fact they are ambiguous. In the end they are as unreal as the Dutch Mountains. Constructing precise differentiations, they have, in fact, taken the perception of surface beyond natural vision.

In the next group of works, the Color Studies, Dibbets used the artificial surfaces of car bodies. These are surfaces without movement and without texture. Because of that there was no point in joining a number of small photographs together in a single, differentiated image. The surface of the car bodies presented instead shining, textureless color.

The works he made consist of three or four panels, each panel showing a single, large photograph. Because the bodies of cars are usually convex, the colors do not appear as even surfaces; they are touched by light and reflections that make them uneven. The forms come close to the surface of the photograph but they do not stay there. This effect is somewhat similar to the vibrating surfaces of the Water Structures. Because the surface varies, the color is not flat, it is strangely at odds with the flat surface and with the square shape of the photographs. It is as if the photograph tries to hold them steady, but the color shapes are restless within the photograph, pulsating within a tight frame.

With the Color Studies Dibbets completed a wide circle of research into the potential of photography as an abstract medium. The search took him from dry transformations in the Perspective Corrections, through various effects that could be produced by manipulating the camera, to a concentration upon surface as structure and, finally, to pure color. The discovery of color was of fundamental importance for Dibbets, and for that reason alone I consider the Color Studies, which have never been greatly appreciated (perhaps because they are formally not spectacular), to be among his major works. Previously he had manipulated perception by imposing formal structures. After The Shortest Day Pieces, color entered his work as simply another element, but hardly more than that. In the Dutch Mountains, but also in the Structure Pieces, the natural presence of color was primarily descriptive and illustrative. In the Color Studies, however, color became the substance of the image itself; and thus the images suggested the use of color as an autonomous element in the construction of works. In fact, when Dibbets made the Color Studies in 1976, for technical reasons he could not go beyond a certain size with each image. Since then, much larger photographic paper has become available, and recently he remade one of the Color Studies on panels two meters square. That work demonstrates that the visual effect aimed at in the smaller Color Studies can be even more powerful when enlarged, without losing its formal tightness.

Still, when they were made, the single photographs in the earliest Color Studies were relatively large. Also they were the most purely visual works Dibbets had made up to that point. The structural component that in other works, for instance the Comets, was paramount, was almost non-existent in the Color Studies, perhaps suggesting that the works could be larger. Because the formal structures used in previous works were relatively intricate, it would have been difficult to enlarge them because in enlargement the coherence of the formal structure could easily disintegrate. Color, on the other hand, can hold large-size surfaces because it has no internal formal structure; it can be used as continuous substance.

After the Color Studies, Dibbets slowly began to make larger work. He created structures that are a combination or a synthesis of several structures he had previously used separately. He began using them in combinations that reinforced them, as in a seminal work called *Structure Panorama 360°* (1977; p. 112). He picked up the "old" 1971 idea of the panoramic survey, combining it with that of the Surface Structures, articulated in the Water Structures. Only this time he chose not an infinitely undifferentiated surface, but a pavement with a distinct geometric pattern and a strong color. Hence the resulting curve, larger than he had made before, is also a strong shape, able to sustain its size. The shape is tight like a muscled arm. To give it more weight on the white ground he began to draw around it. He had done this previously but only occasionally when a shape that threatened to slide off the paper needed some structural reinforcement. From then on, drawing around the photographic shape became a strategy, also aimed at articulating the difference between abstract pattern and photographic shape.

From there he went on, arriving, in 1979, at a still larger and grander formulation of the panorama principle. In making works like *Structure Panorama 360°* he encountered two problems. Occasionally they tended to be slightly descriptive as surfaces, lacking the marvelous ambiguity of the Color Studies, and there was the practical fact that in photographing pavements and floors, the height of the tripod imposed a limit, reducing flexibility.

In a major work of 1979, *Construction 330°* (p. 43), he avoided these problems in the actual construction of the image. The "trick" was simple and effective: he turned the curved shape upside down, heightening its appearance as an abstract shape of color; and, in order to hold that shape he mounted it on a semicircular panel. The effect is one of a strange lightness. The eye, which in the earlier panoramas automatically centers on the surface, seeing it as pavement on which one can walk, no longer finds a point of reference or rest. This effect was new in Dibbets's work. In almost all of the previous work, the eye is framed by the formal power of the construction, forms of perception are imposed upon natural vision. In *Construction 330°* the eye is left to wander. It was with this change in perceptual mode that the later architectural panoramas began, those sometimes identified with the name of the Dutch painter Saenredam. Saenredam had, like Dibbets, looked at architecture as though it were a still life, and then painted the interior of churches like atmospheric landscapes.

Construction 330° showed a pavement upside down, as if it were a ceiling. Next, because it liberated the camera from the height of the tripod, giving him more freedom of movement, Dibbets photographed the beamed ceiling of a room in a Tuscan farm and reconstructed it as a panorama. Doing that, a new problem made itself manifest, or rather an old problem reemerged. How does a photographic shape, a construction, fit on the paper or panel supporting it? To what extent must it appear as construction, to what extent as image from which the structural component fades away? Once again in his work Dibbets had to make that vital choice.

Let us go back for a moment to *Structure Panorama 360°*. In that work the constructed, curved shape sits on the white ground as what it is, a pavement. The shape has a certain weight which is further articulated by the drawing around it. That drawing reiterates or echoes the structural character of the photographic shape. The weight of the shape also coincides with the camera's downward view; one's own view stops with the shape on the paper. But looking at a ceiling one looks upward. This changes completely the visual character of a work such as *San Casciano Ceiling* (1979; p. 131).

In all his previous work Dibbets had shaped perception, sometimes giving it ambiguous twists, but there had always been a precise and discrete relationship with the natural ways of seeing. There was a fine difference between the two kinds of perception, but never a complete, illogical cut. But constructing a panorama of a ceiling on a white ground was such a cut, because the constructed shape appeared as too heavy. In the "miniature" form of the preparatory study the construction was still acceptable. In making a larger version, however, Dibbets found that he had to introduce color. Embedding the constructed photographic shape in a soft field of color made it appear lighter. By relating that color to the color of the photographs he could make the sharp edges of the photographs disappear. But he did not apply color with a paintbrush. Using very liquid pigments, inks and watercolors, he washed the paper surface of the panel, time and time again, thus softening the surface of the paper itself. The paper became, instead of the support for color, a field of color, strong in hue but also transparent, like the sky. In this expanse of color the constructed form appears as a strange concentration, sometimes as a shape drawing the color toward itself, making the entire surface taut and tense. The photographic shape is like an apparition within the color field, the whole a blended image of great visual distinction and power.

In Dibbets's art there has always been a strong sense of logic. The artistic decisions he has made have always been reasonable interventions; that is, they were interventions into an ongoing process of artistic reasoning. Steps that were taken to slightly change the direction of his art did not interrupt its vital, internal continuity. The change, for instance, from the constructed paintings and the small earth constructions to the Perspective Corrections in 1967 was more a change in expression and concentration than a fundamental change in artistic reasoning. The Perspective Corrections—discovering photography as a means of formal articulation—were able to pinpoint a particular effect in the earlier works (optical change of shape by change of position) and to isolate that effect and develop its visual potential in isolation. Changes of "image" in Dibbets's work have always been logical; he takes elements or clues from previous work and carries them to their next stage in which they may change almost completely.

A photograph is an image isolated from reality, separated forever from the visual totality of which it was a part. It is working with such isolated fragments that gives Dibbets's art, at the same time, extraordinary tightness and flexibility. An isolated fragment may be handled or manipulated freely, because it has been taken out of its context and has become rootless: although "realistic" by nature, because of its linguistic isolation it is extremely abstract. Dibbets may then consider and contemplate these photographic elements that are at the center of his work, and he may give their appearance any possible twist he likes. There, however, his "Dutch" sense of precision comes in. The changes from "image" to "image" are always measured and they have a precise sense of purpose. Invention follows invention, each visual phase is clearly marked and recognizable, but an image is never exhausted in a dogmatic, conceptual way, because it is Dibbets's deepest conviction that it is the artist's business to keep images alive, to carry them through time.

Dibbets's concern is with images, images close to us, not those that are remote. Therefore, his relationships to historical art (Saenredam, Monet, Mondrian) come through his interest in images, of whatever era, that are still alive, waiting to be used again. His concern is not with theory but with forms of articulation of certain visual effects that remain open-ended, that could, so to speak, fit the next form. Dibbets makes works that keep alive his previous inventions, and he has developed certain very flexible strategic (linguistic) structures that he can follow separately (as in the Perspective Corrections or Dutch Mountains or Color Studies) or use in combination (Panoramas or Saenredam Pieces) clearly and precisely.

Dibbets's greatest skill is his ability to arrange a miracle from which construction fades away. His first works originated within the general context of Minimal and so-called Conceptual Art; that aesthetic provided the general framework of his thinking and certainly alerted him to a particular kind of work. But his sensibility was always pictorial, and almost from the beginning he formulated his works not as constructions or concepts but as images—even as paintings.

The detached image, floating in its field of hues and veils as deep as the sky, is immensely flexible; it can freely, imaginatively move in its space, as earlier photographic images could not. The Perspective Corrections came into being through a single, swift movement, and later works, notably the Dutch Mountain and the Comet series, rely on precisely measured movement, or movement brought to a specific halt. Their power as perceptual constructions lies in their gently controlled transformations; these images seem to be arrested in the course of their movement. Transformations between two states—namely the beginning and the end—make these constructions clear, precise and readable within their own terms. In the most recent works the image continues to move, turning around its structure, literally like a ship slowly drifting on a sea of hazy color. This gesture represents a significant move toward the pictorial in Dibbets's work, promising a whole new range of possibilities.

(overleaf)
Jan Dibbets's studio,
Amsterdam 1981

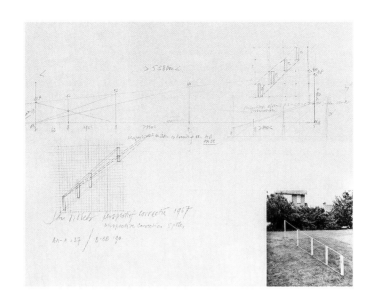

**Perspective Correction,
5 Poles** 1967
black and white photograph
and pencil on paper
20 x 25½
50 x 65
Private collection

**Perspective Correction,
Square with 2 Diagonals**
1968
black and white photograph
with negative and pencil
on paper
20 x 25½
50 x 65
Private collection

**Perspective Correction,
Horizontal, Vertical,
Cross** 1968
black and white photographs
and pencil on paper
20 x 25½
50 x 65
Private collection

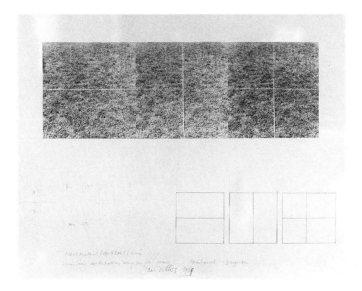

**Two Cones with Green
Connection**   1968
papier-mâché, neon
33 x 69 x 51¼
84 x 175 x 130
Collection Stedelijk Museum,
Amsterdam

Installation at Konrad Fischer's
Gallery, Düsseldorf   1968
faggots, neon, sand, mud

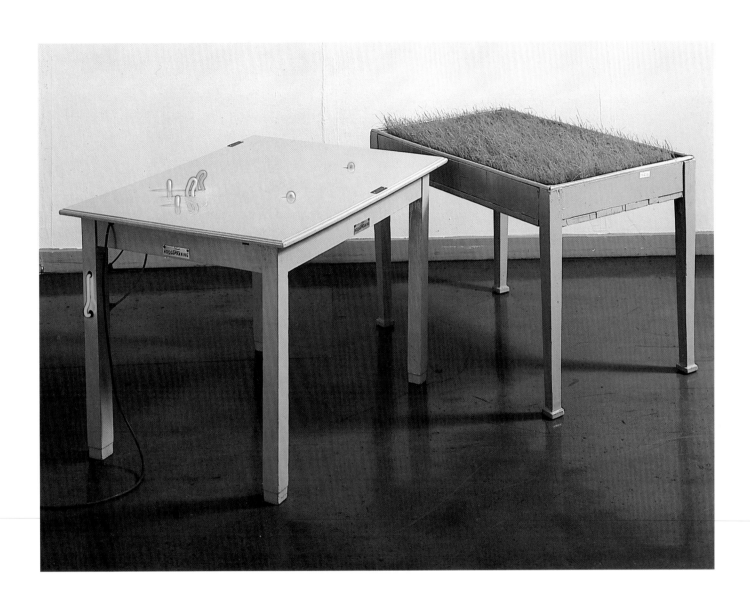

**Grass Table and Neon
Table**   1968
wood, grass, neon
Grass Table: 29 x 27½ x 43¼
74 x 70 x 110
Neon Table: 29½ x 33½ x 43¼
75 x 85 x 110
Private collection,
on extended loan to the
Kunstmuseum, Lucerne

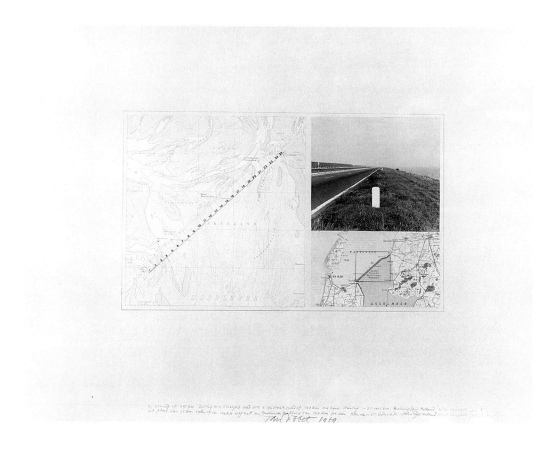

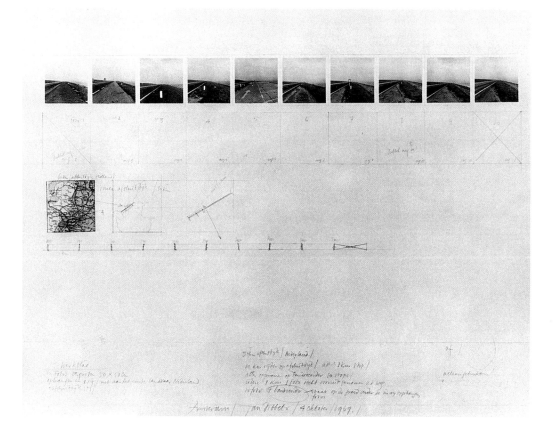

**The Sound of 25 km.,
Holland** 1969
black and white photograph,
maps, adhesive digits and
pencil on paper and cassette
(sound)
22 x 30
56 x 76
Collection Gian Enzo Sperone

**Study for Afsluitdijk,
10 km.** 1969
black and white photographs,
map and pencil on paper
29½ x 39½
75 x 100
Collection Agnes and
Frits Becht

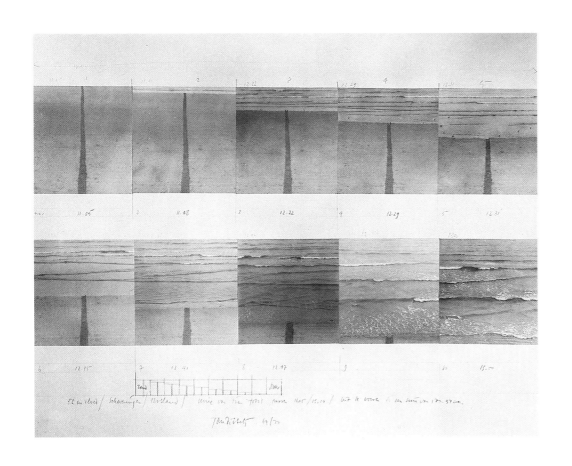

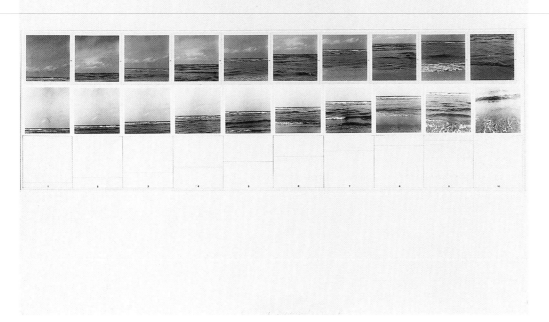

Flood Tide, Sketch after the Work 1969–1970
black and white photographs
and pencil on paper
27½ x 35½
70 x 90
Collection Von der
Heydt-Museum, Wuppertal

Horizon, Sea 1971
color and black and white
photographs, stickers and
pencil on paper
32 x 37
81 x 94
Private collection

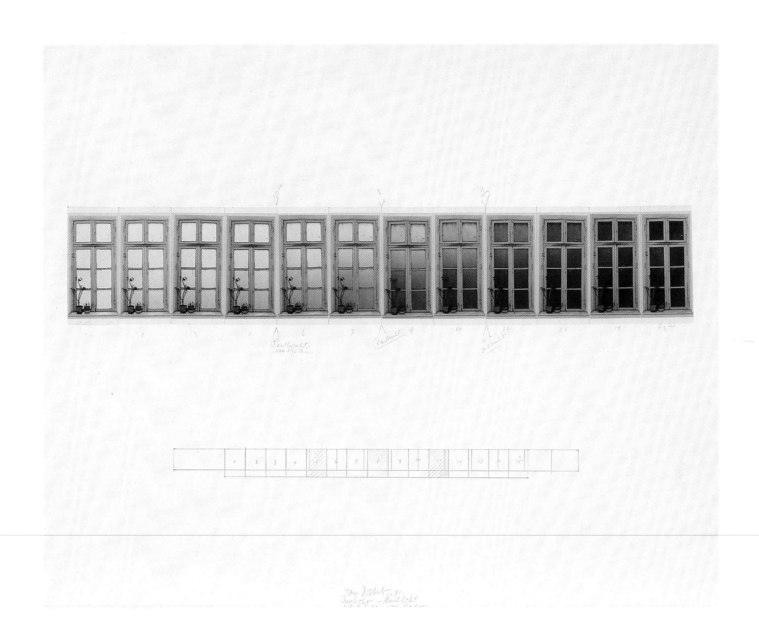

**Daylight, Flashlight
Outside Light, Inside
Light** 1971
color photographs
and pencil on paper
20 x 25½
50 x 65
Private collection

(opposite)
**The Shortest Day at Konrad
Fischer's Gallery** 1970
color photographs on board
69 x 71
175 x 180
Collection FER

Venetian Blind 1971–1972
color photographs on paper
46¾ x 27
118.5 x 69
Collection Agrati, Milan

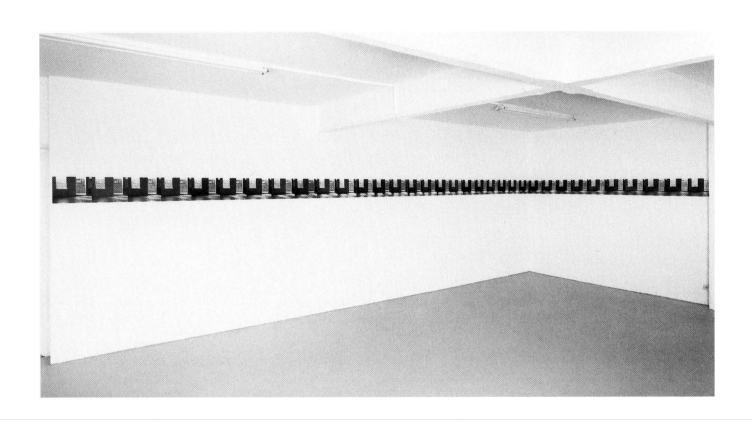

**The Shadows in My
Studio** 1969
black and white photographs
on cardboard
9 x 407½
23 x 1035
Collection Anton and
Annick Herbert
(Installation view)

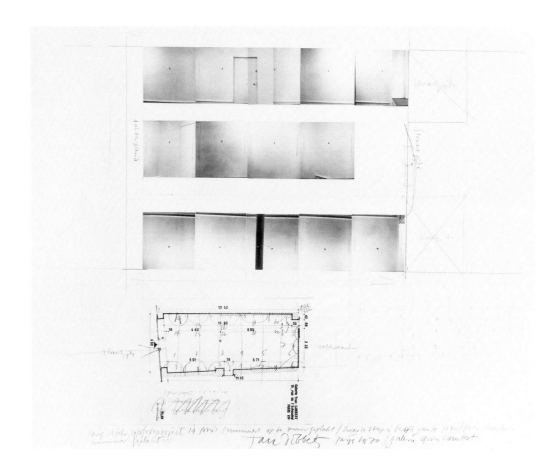

**Numbers on Wall A
(Gallery Yvon Lambert,
Paris)** 1970
black and white photographs,
floor plan of the gallery and
pencil on paper
29½ x 35½
75 x 90
Collection Daled

**Numbers on Wall B
(Gallery Françoise Lambert,
Milan)** 1970
black and white photographs,
floor plan of the gallery and
pencil on paper
29½ x 39½
75 x 100
Collection Angelo Baldassarre

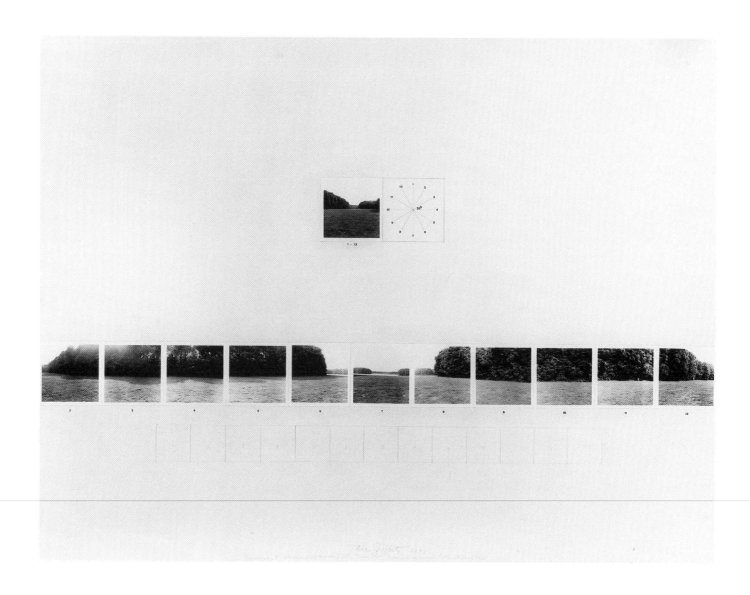

**Panorama, Amsterdamse
Bos I** 1971
black and white photographs,
adhesive digits
and pencil on paper
29½ x 39½
75 x 100
Collection Peder Bonnier

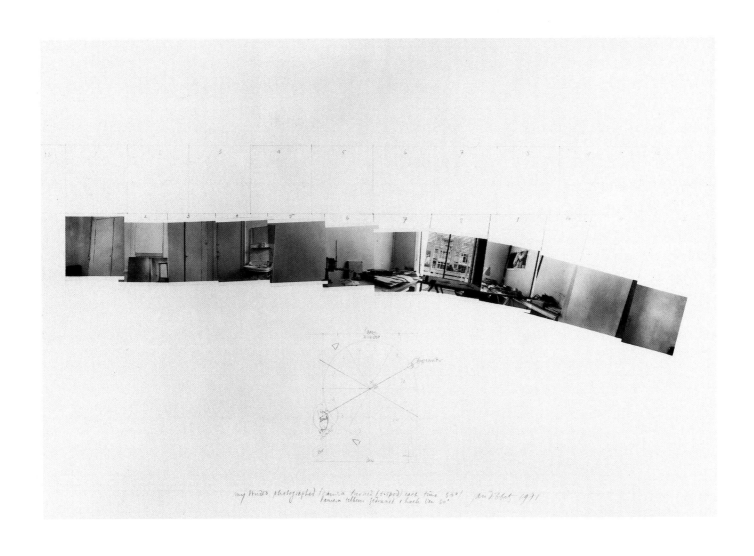

Panorama, My Studio   1971
black and white photographs
and pencil on paper
26¼ x 38
66.5 x 96
Collection Stedeljik Museum,
Amsterdam

**Big Panorama,
Amsterdamse Bos** 1971
color photographs on
aluminum
17¾ x 196¾
45 x 500

**Panorama, Amsterdamse
Bos** 1971
black and white and color
photographs and pencil
on paper
29½ x 39½
75 x 100
Private collection
(Installation view)

Panorama Dutch
Mountain, 12 x 15°
Sea II A 1971
color photographs
and pencil on paper
29½ x 39½
75 x 100
Collection Trustees of
the Tate Gallery, London

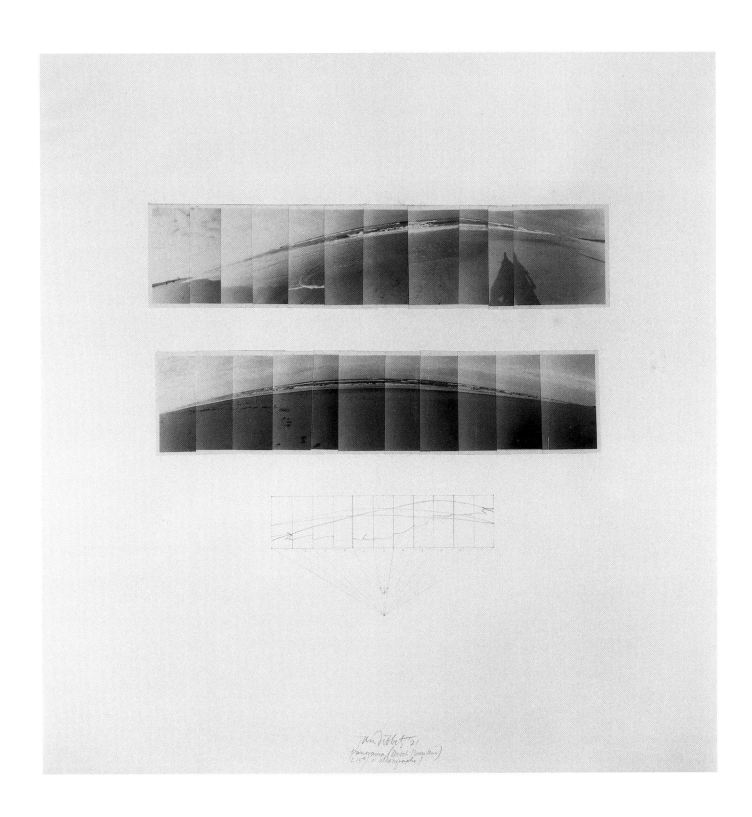

Panorama Dutch
Mountain, Sea 1971
color photographs
and pencil on paper
28 x 27¾
71 x 70.5
Collection Panza di Biumo

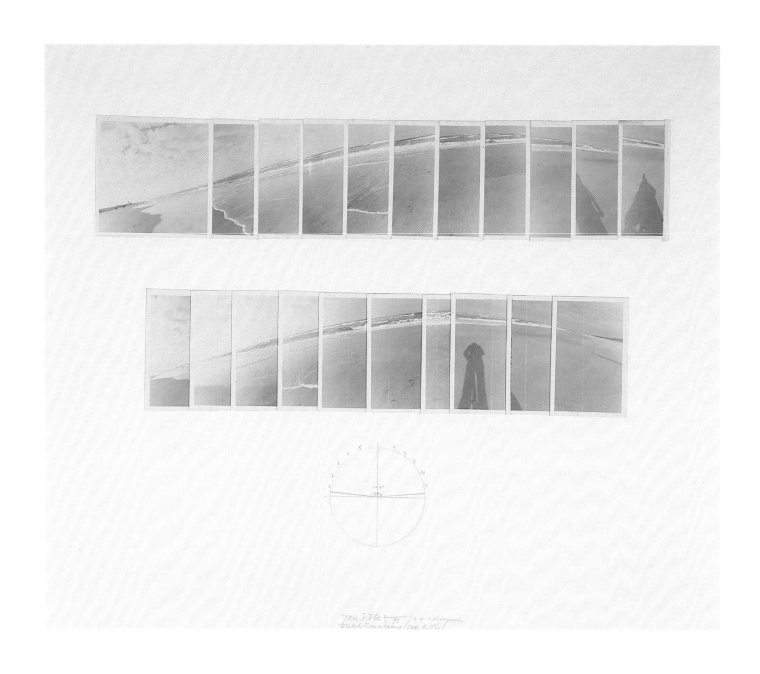

**Dutch Mountain, Sea
Hills** 1971
color photographs and
pencil on paper
19¾ x 27¼
50.6 x 69
Collection Australian National
Gallery, Canberra

**Panorama Dutch
Mountain, Land**   1971
color photographs on
aluminum
18¼ x 179
46.5 x 455

**Panorama Dutch
Mountain, Land**   1971
color photographs and
pencil on paper
29½ x 39½ each of four
75 x 100
Collection Crex, Hallen für
neue Kunst, Schaffhausen
(Installation view)

Dutch Mountain,
Big Sea I 'A' 1971
eleven color photographs
on aluminum
34 x 179
86 x 454.5

Study for Dutch Mountain,
Sea I 'A' 1971
color photographs
and pencil on paper
29½ x 39½
75 x 100
Collection The Museum
of Modern Art, New York
Purchase. 150.73a–f.
(Installation view)

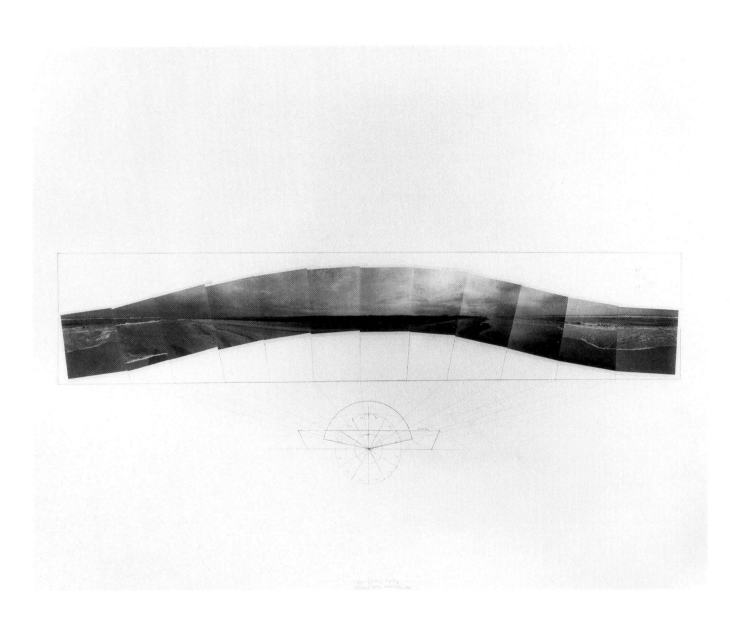

**Collapsed Dutch Mountain,
Sea** 1972
color photographs
and pencil on paper
26¼ x 35½
69 x 90
Private collection

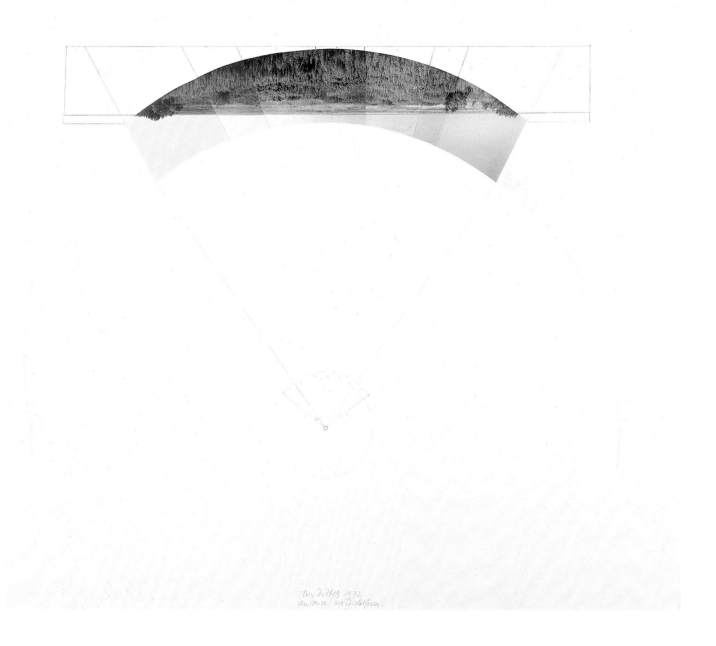

**Universe, World's
Platform** 1972
color photographs
and pencil on paper
25½ x 25½
65 x 65
Collection Stedelijk Museum,
Amsterdam

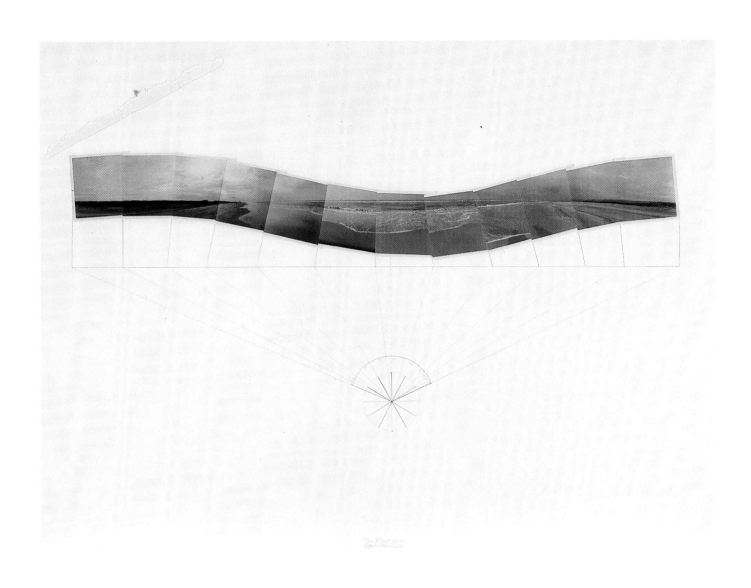

**Negative Mountain,
Sea** 1972
color photographs
and pencil on paper
27¼ x 38
69 x 96
Collection Mrs. Nono
de Wilde-Reinhold

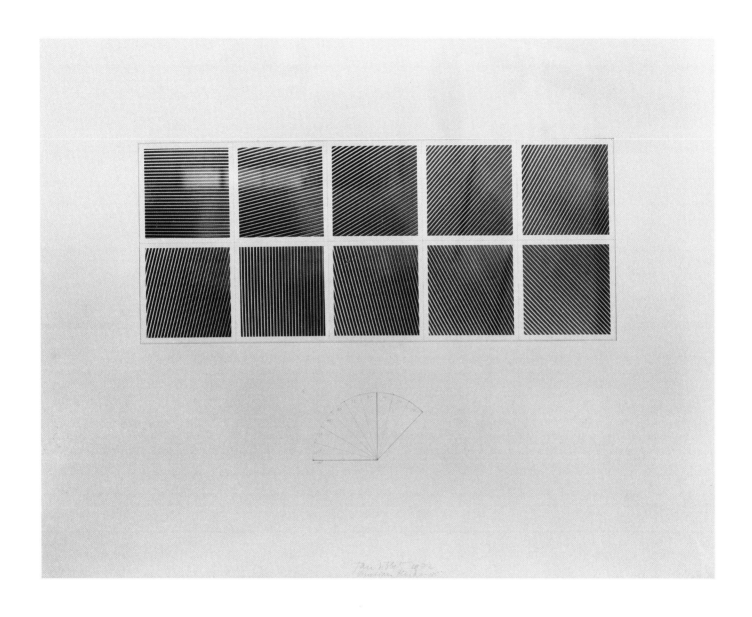

0°–135° Venetian
Blind 1972
black and white photographs
and pencil on paper
20 x 25½
50 x 65
Private collection

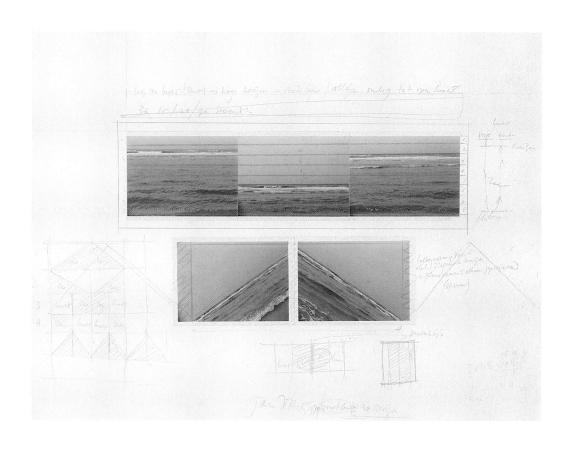

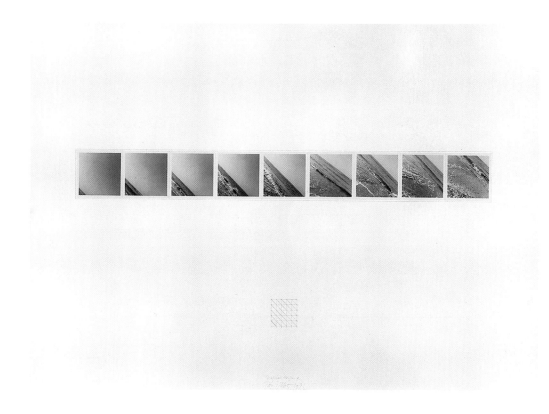

**Study for Film Horizon
3 x 45°** 1970
color photographs
and pencil on paper
16 x 22
41 x 56
Private collection

Horizon, Sea 45° 1971
color photographs
and pencil on paper
27½ x 39½
70 x 100
Private collection

Land, Horizon 0°–135°
1972
color photographs
on aluminum
19¾ x 197
50 x 500
Collection Anton and Annick
Herbert, on extended loan to
the Stedelijk Van
Abbemuseum, Eindhoven
(Installation view)

Sectio Aurea 1972
color photographs
and pencil on paper
33½ x 41½
85 x 105
Collection Haags
Gemeentemuseum

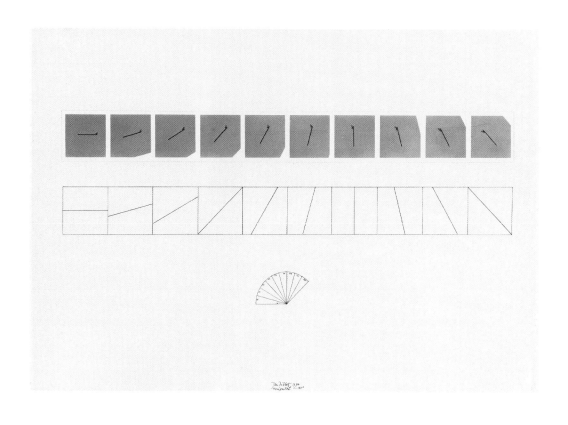

0°–135° Horizontal 1972
black and white photographs
and pencil on paper
27½ x 39½
70 x 100
Collection Geert-Jan Visser on
extended loan to
Rijksmuseum Kröller-Müller,
Otterlo

Sea Horizon 0°–135° 1972
color photographs
and pencil on paper
26½ x 38
67.5 x 97
Private collection

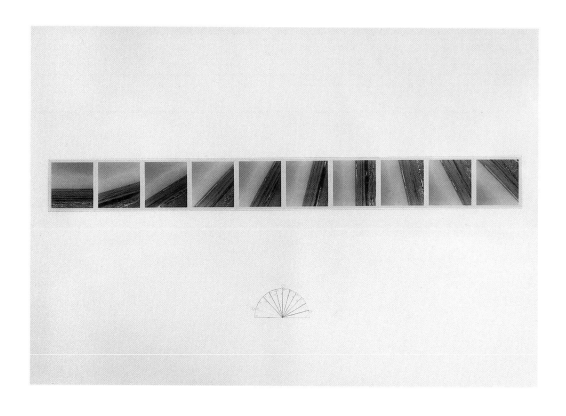

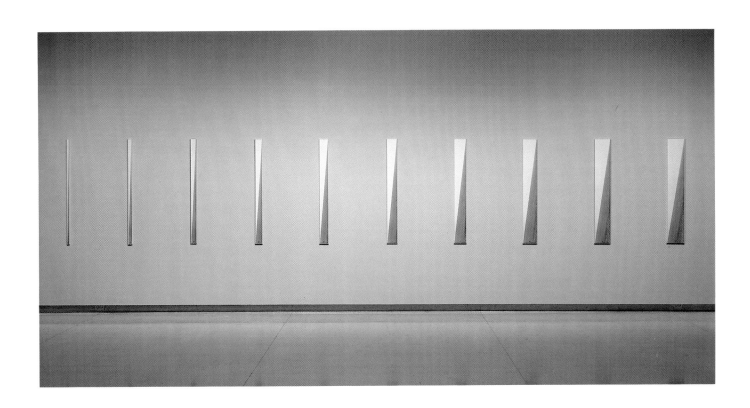

Horizon 1°–10° Land   1973
ten color photographs
48 x variable width
Collection Walker Art Center,
Minneapolis, Art Center
Acquisition Fund, 1978
(Installation view)

**Comet Horizon 6°–72°,
Sky/Sea/Sky**   1973
twelve individually framed
color photographs
122 x 113
310 x 287.5
Private collection
(Installation view)

**Construction of Sea
3°–60°/9°–81°**   1973
color photographs
and pencil on paper
29½ x 37½
75 x 95
Whereabouts unknown

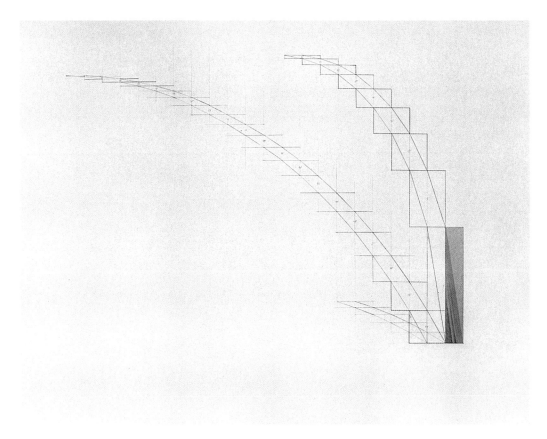

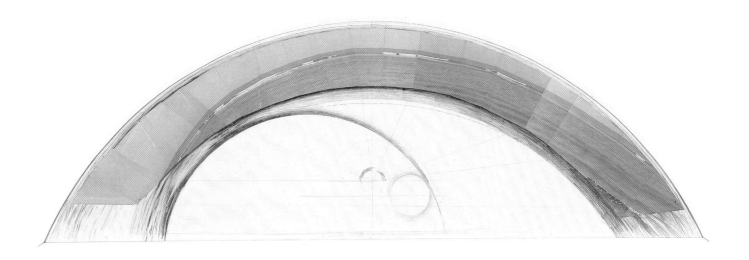

Untitled 1973
color photographs
and pencil on paper
mounted on chipboard
23¾ x 72¼
60.5 x 183.5
Private collection

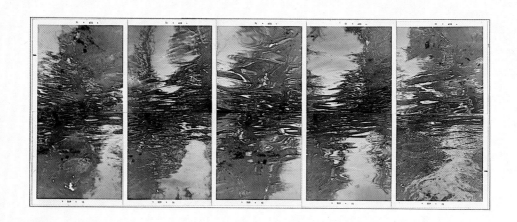

**1st Study for Monet's
Dream** 1973
color photographs on paper
20 x 25½
50 x 65
Collection Hester van Royen

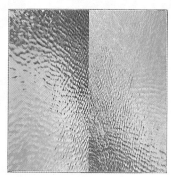

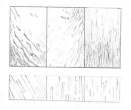

Waterstructure 1975
color photographs
and pencil on paper
29 x 35¼
74.5 x 89.5
Collection Art Gallery of South
Australia, Adelaide

Monet's Dream
Study 1975
color photographs on paper
28¾ x 40
73 x 102
Collection Stedelijk Museum,
Amsterdam

Reeds 1973
color photographs on paper
23½ x 67¾
60 x 172
Private collection

Structure Piece 1974
color photographs
and pencil on paper
mounted on board
17¹¹⁄₁₆ x 102
45 x 259
Private collection

Structure Study   1974
color photographs
and pencil on paper
20 x 25½
50 x 65
Private collection

Structure Piece 1974
color photographs
and pencil on paper
105½ x 13¾
267.9 x 35
Private collection

Waterstructure S.C.D.B.
1975
color photographs
and pencil on paper
27½ x 43½
70 x 110
Collection Angelo Baldassarre

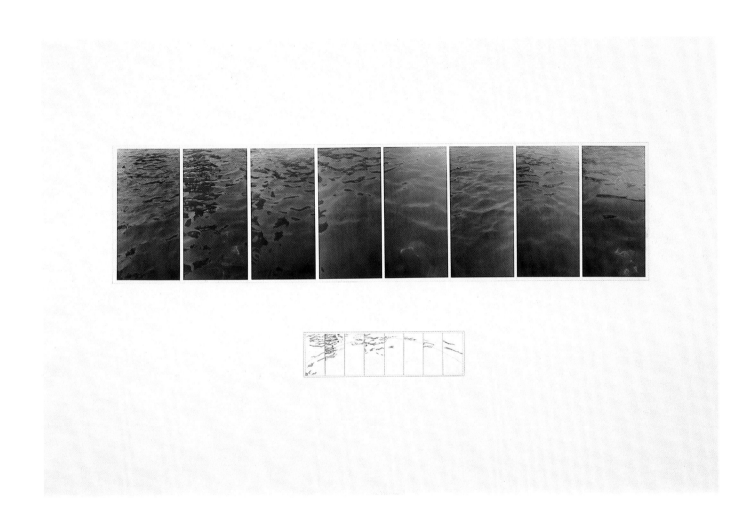

Waterstructure 1975
color photographs
and pencil on paper
27 x 43½
69 x 110
Collection Gianfranco
Dioguardi

(overleaf)
Colorstudy H1, 2, 3, 4
1976–1985
color photographs
69 x 69 each of four
175 x 175
Private collection
(Installation view)

Black and White Structure,
No. 4 1978
black and white photographs
and pencil on paper
31½ x 43½
80 x 110
Collection Australian National
Gallery, Canberra

**Black and White
Structure** 1978
black and white photographs
and pencil on paper
31½ x 43½
80 x 110
Private collection

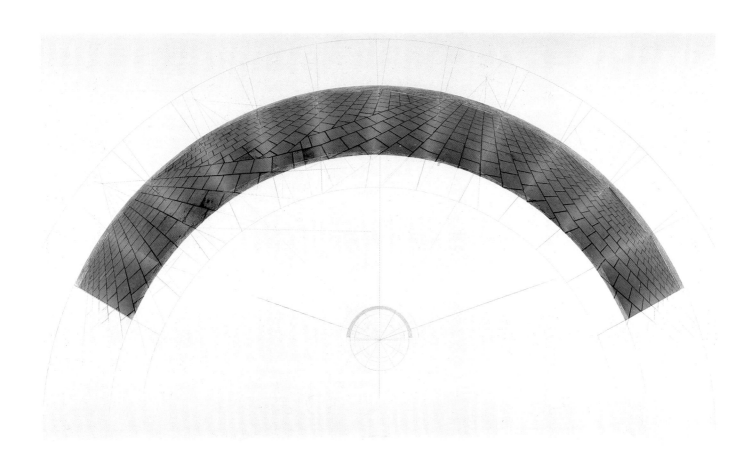

Structure Panorama
360° 1977
color photographs and
pencil on paper
mounted on polystyrene board
34 x 57¾
86.5 x 146.5
Collection Morton G.
Neumann Family

**Self-portrait as
Photographer** 1981
color photographs and
pencil on paper
mounted on chipboard
73 x 73
185 x 185
Collection Mike and
Penny Winton

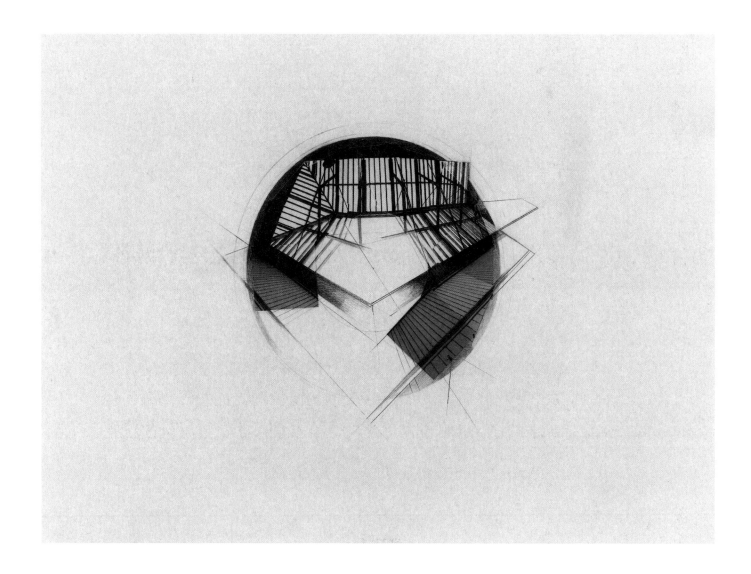

Guinness Hopstore
Dublin 1983
color photographs
and pencil on card
28¾ x 40
73 x 102
Collection Richard
and Gail Elden

114

Guinness Hopstore
Dublin 1984–1986
color photographs, watercolor
and pencil on paper
mounted on chipboard
55¼ x 73
140 x 185
Private collection

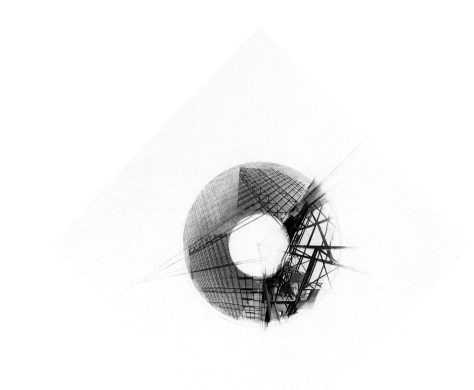

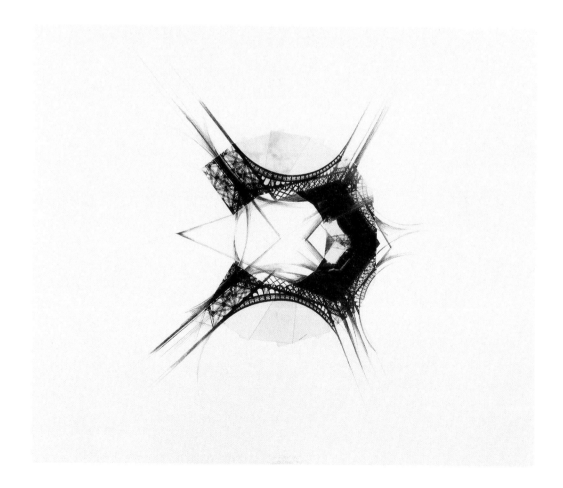

GdN Rotterdam 1981
color photographs
and pencil on card
28¾ x 28¾
73 x 73
Courtesy Waddington
Galleries, London

Eiffeltower 1981
color photographs
and pencil on paper
28¾ x 34
73 x 86
Collection Joan S. Sonnabend

Hommage à Apollinaire
1982–1984
color photographs, watercolor
and glass-pencil on paper
mounted on chipboard
73 x 72½
185 x 184
Collection Exxon Corporation

Orvieto II 1982
color photographs and
pencil on paper
mounted on chipboard
73 x 73
185 x 185
Collection Vance E. Kondon
and Liesbeth Giesberger

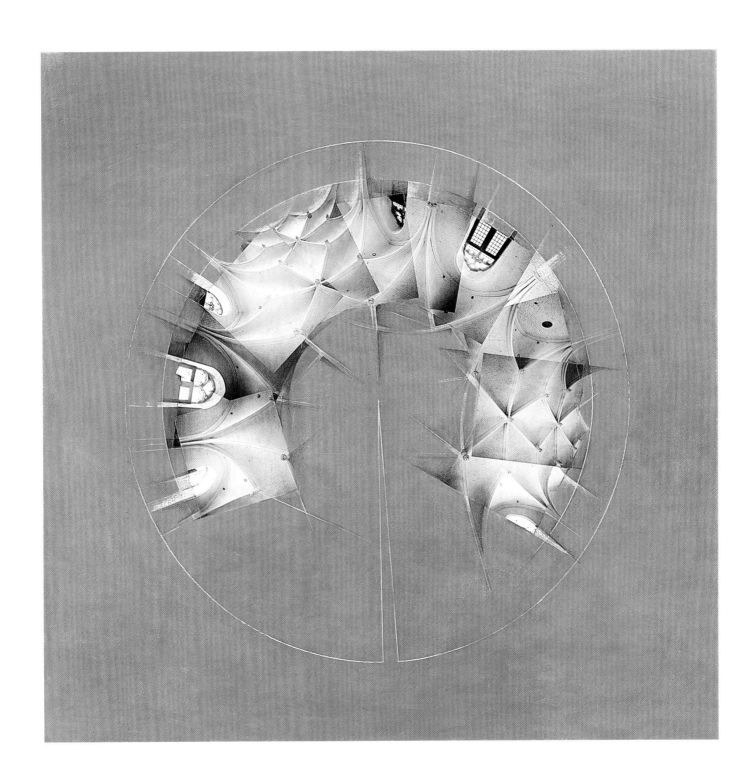

Middelburg 1982–1983
color photographs, watercolor
and glass-pencil on paper
mounted on chipboard
72½ x 73
184 x 185
Collection The Art Museum
of the Ateneum, Helsinki

Four Courts Dublin   1984
color photographs and
watercolor on paper
mounted on chipboard
49¼ x 61
125 x 155
Collection Bayer USA Inc.

Four Courts Dublin
1983–1984
color photographs,
watercolor, pencil and
glass-pencil on paper
mounted on chipboard
49¼ x 61
125 x 155
Collection Joan S. Sonnabend

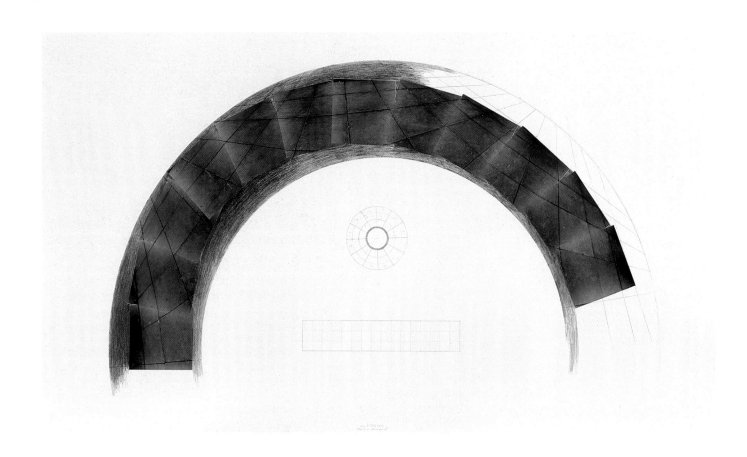

Structure Panorama
360° 1977
color photographs and
pencil on paper mounted on
polystyrene board
31½ x 55¼
80 x 140
Collection Louisiana Museum
of Modern Art, Humlebaek

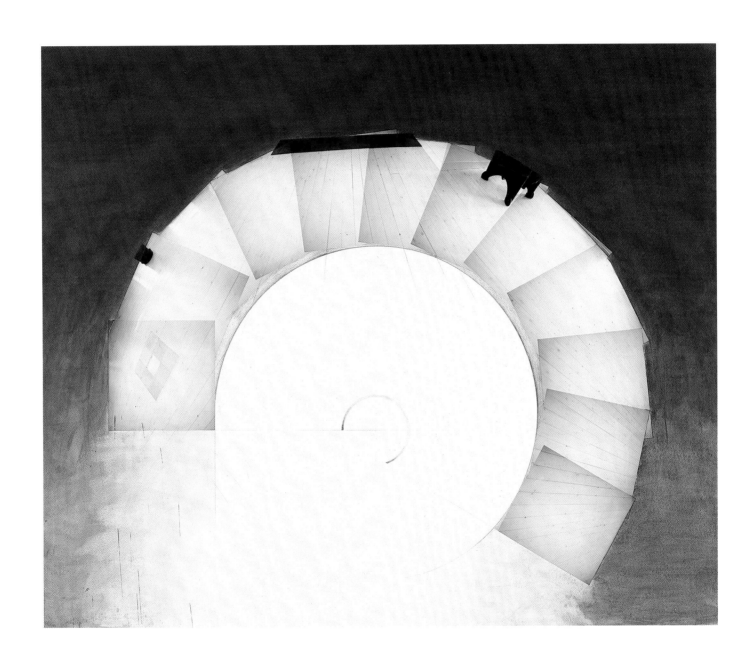

Kosmos 1984
color photographs, watercolor
and pencil on paper
mounted on chipboard
73 x 88½
185 x 225
Private collection

Vondelpark 1979
black and white photographs
and pencil on paper
28 x 28½
71 x 72
Collection Mrs. Sao
Schlumberger

Vondelpark   1980
color photographs and
pencil on paper
mounted on cardboard
28¾ x 40
75 x 102
Collection Hannelore B.
Schulhof

Vondelpark 360° 1980
color photographs and
pencil on paper
mounted on chipboard
51 x 67
130 x 170
Collection Mike and
Penny Winton

126

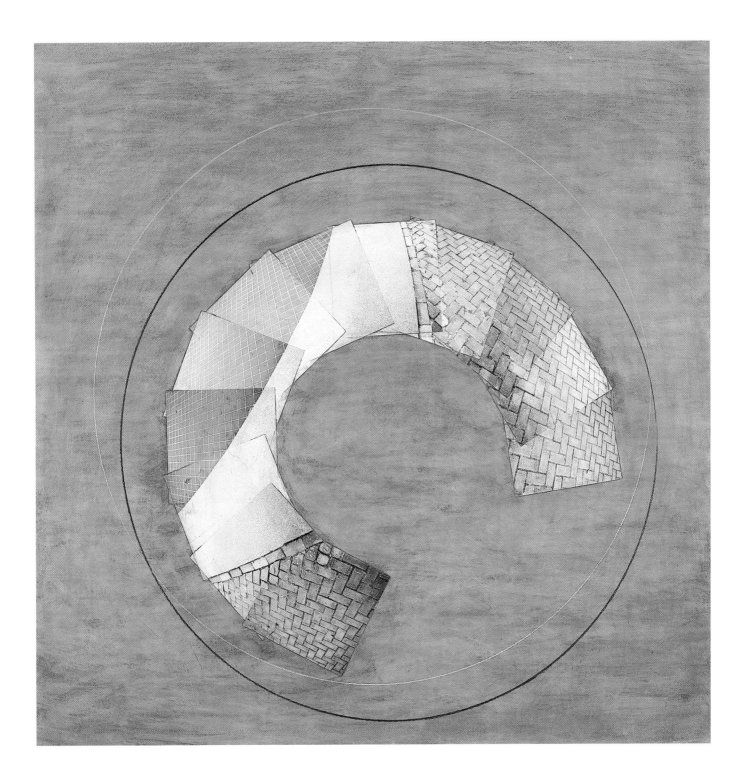

Vondelpark II   1984–1985
color photographs,
watercolor, pencil and
glass-pencil on paper
mounted on chipboard
73 x 73
185 x 185
Collection
Bonnefantenmuseum,
Maastricht

Spoleto Duomo   1980
black and white photographs,
watercolor and glass-pencil
on paper
mounted on chipboard
73 x 88½
185 x 225
Collection Academia
Foundation, Venice

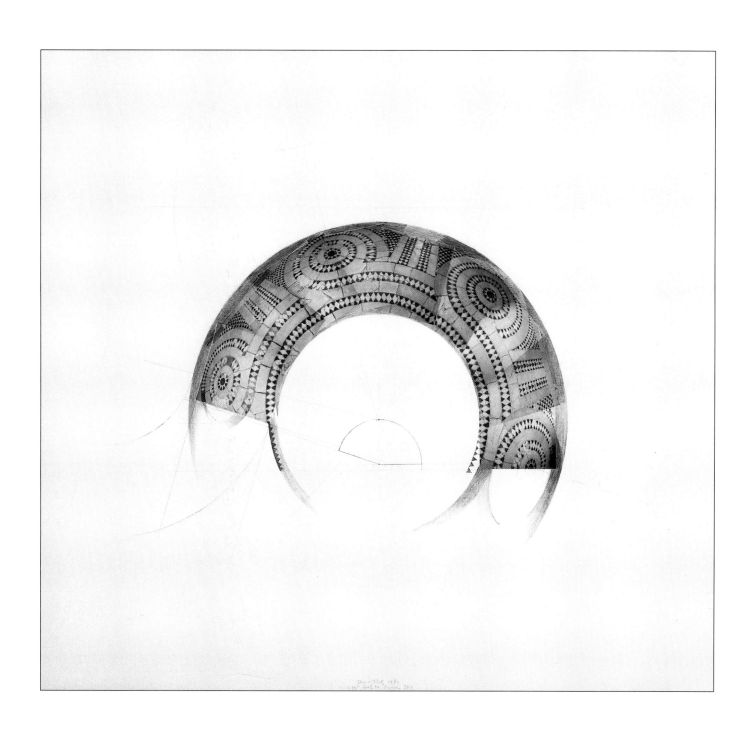

Spoleto Duomo 270° 1980
black and white photographs
and pencil on paper
28 x 31¾
71 x 80.5
Collection Musée de Toulon

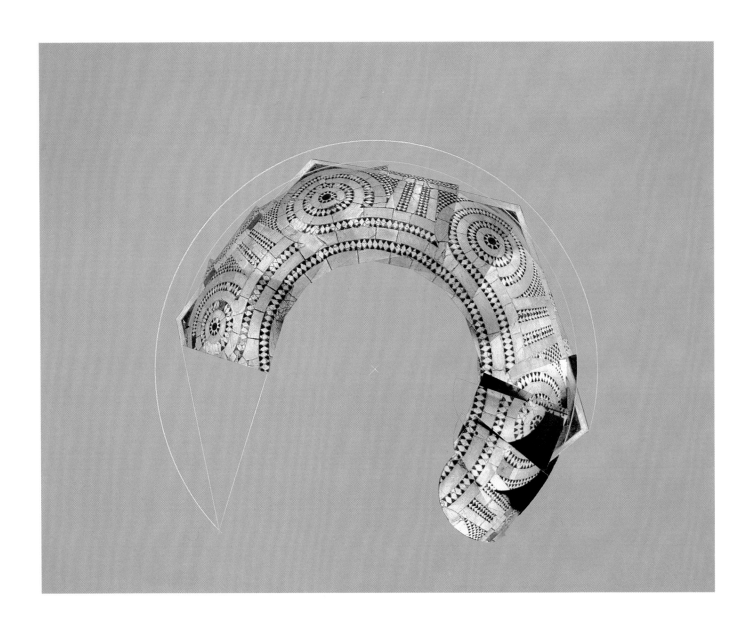

Spoleto Floor 1981
black and white photographs,
acrylic paint and glass-pencil
on paper
mounted on chipboard
51¼ x 69
130 x 175
Collection Museo d'arte
contemporanea,
Castello di Rivoli, Turin

San Casciano Ceiling   1979
color photographs
and pencil on paper
28¾ x 28¾
73 x 73
Collection Mr. and Mrs. Robert
J. Dodds III

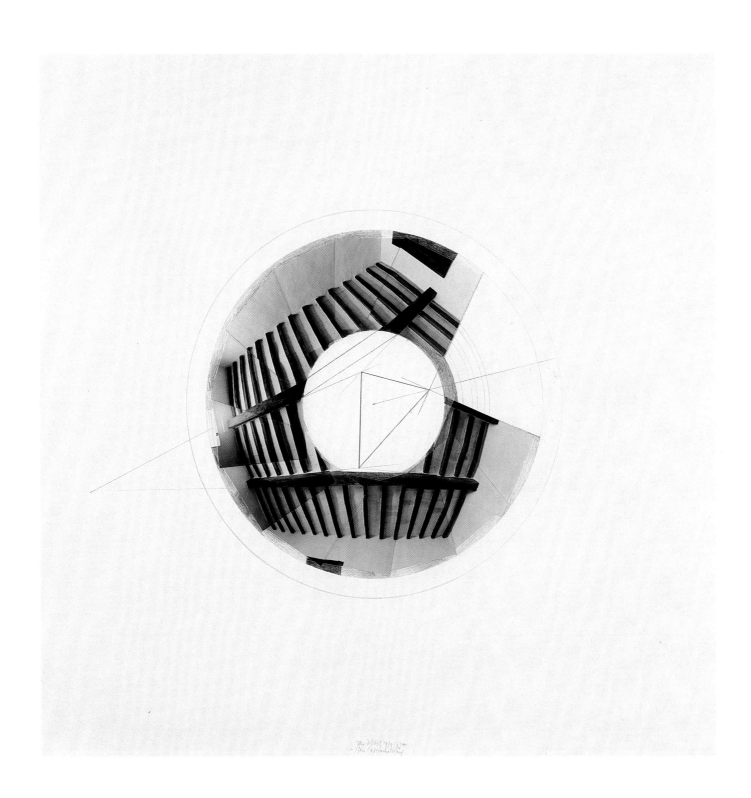

San Casciano Ceiling 1979
color photographs
and pencil on paper
28¾ x 28¾
73 x 73
Collection Hamburger
Kunsthalle

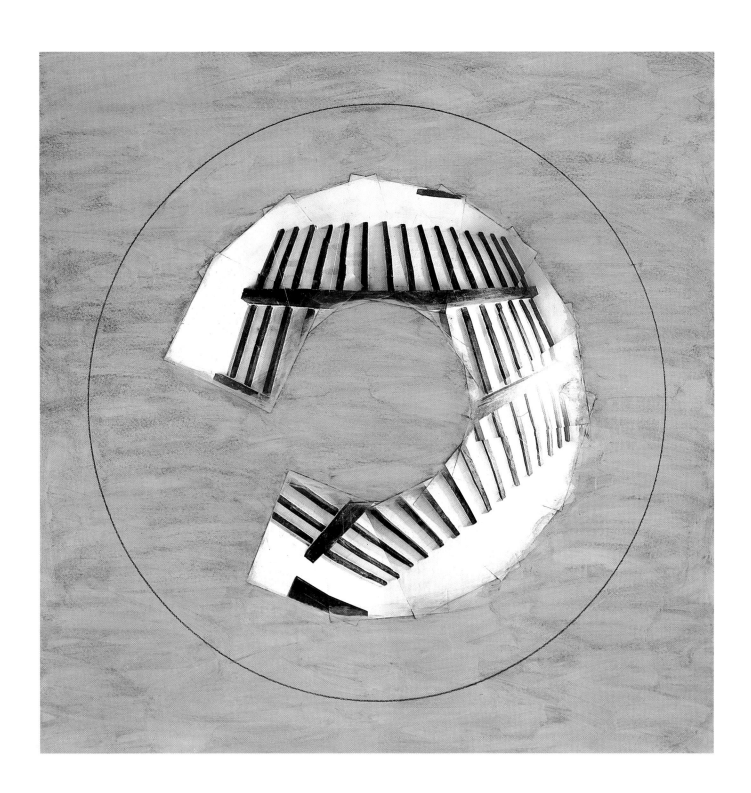

San Casciano Ceiling
1983–1985
color photographs, watercolor
and pencil on paper
mounted on chipboard
73 x 72½
185 x 184
Private collection

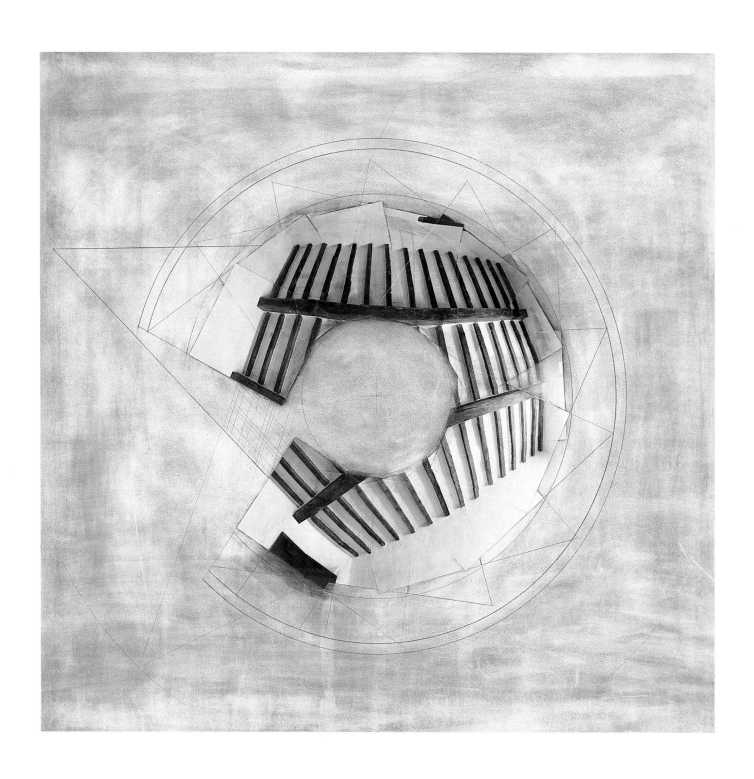

San Casciano Ceiling 1979
color photographs, washed
pencil and pencil on paper
mounted on chipboard
51¼ x 49½
130 x 126
Collection Hiske Dibbets

San Casciano Ceiling
1983–1984
color photographs,
watercolor on paper
mounted on chipboard
73 x 73 each of three
185 x 185
Private collection
(Installation view)

**Round Lutheran
Church** 1985
color photographs and pencil
on paper
mounted on chipboard
72½ x 72½
184 x 184
Collection Sonnabend Estate

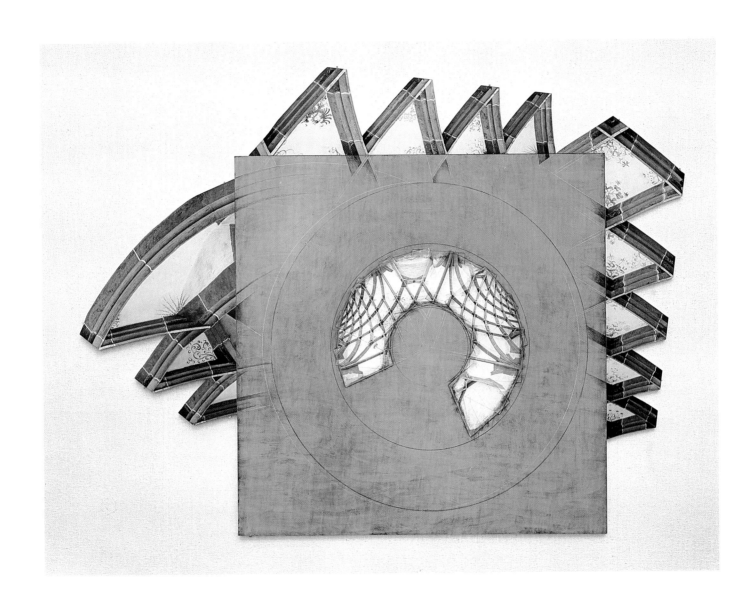

Maulbronn 1983–1985
color photographs,
watercolor, pencil and
glass-pencil on paper
mounted on chipboard
89¼ x 120
227 x 305
Collection Stedelijk Museum,
Amsterdam
(Installation view)

Octagon Triptych   1982
color photographs, watercolor
and pencil on paper
mounted on chipboard
73 x 73 each of three
185 x 185
Private collection
(Installation view)

Octagon I 1982
color photographs, watercolor
and pencil on paper
mounted on chipboard
73 x 73
185 x 185
Collection Solomon R.
Guggenheim Museum,
New York, Purchased with
funds contributed by General
Felt Industries, Inc., 1984

Vondelkerk 1986
color photographs, watercolor
and pencil on paper
mounted on chipboard
60 x 49¼
152 x 125
Collection Vance E. Kondon
and Liesbeth Giesberger

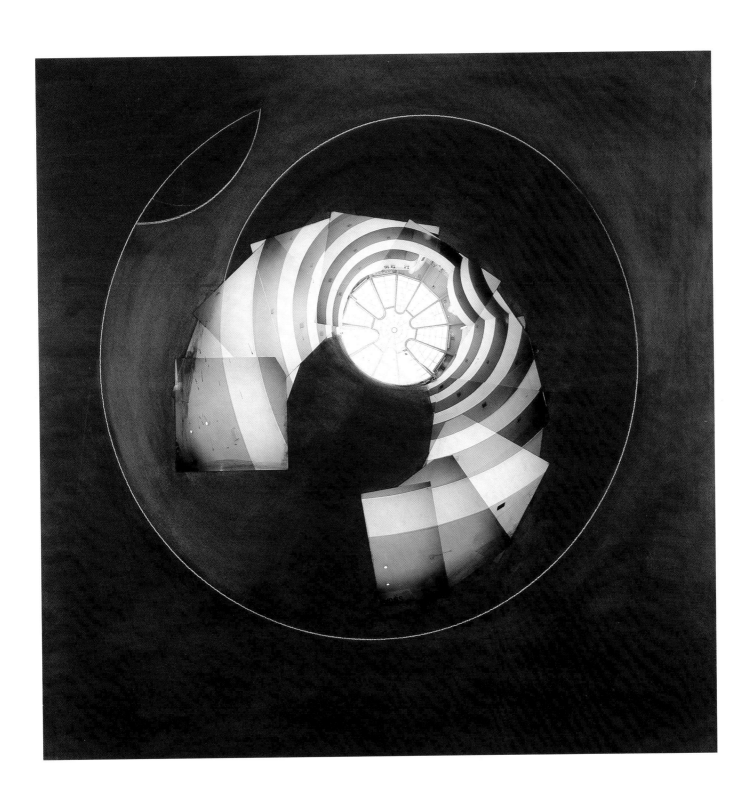

Guggenheim 1986
color photographs, watercolor
and glass-pencil on paper
mounted on chipboard
73 x 73
185 x 185
Private collection

Claustra I 1986
color photographs and
watercolor on paper
mounted on chipboard
72½ x 72½
184 x 184
Collection Stedelijk Van
Abbemuseum, Eindhoven

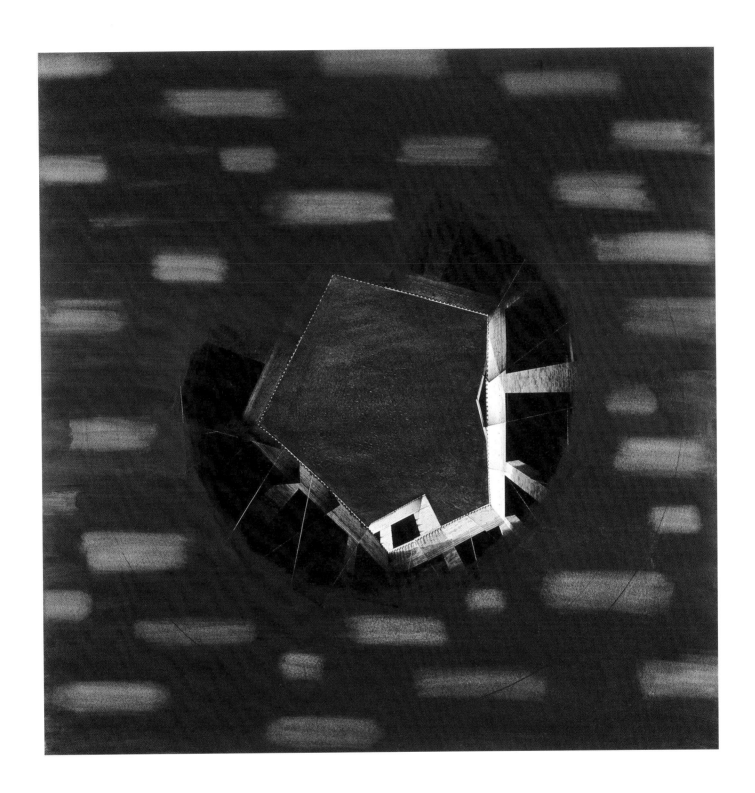

Claustra II   1986
color photographs and
watercolor on paper
mounted on chipboard
73 x 73
185 x 185
Collection Mr. and Mrs.
H. Wyss

Biography

1941
Born in Weert on 9 May.
1959–1963
Training as art teacher at the Academie voor Beeldende en Bouwende Kunsten in Tilburg.
1961–1963
Painting lessons from Jan Gregoor in Eindhoven.
1964
Lives and works in Antwerp.
1964–1967
Lives and works as a teacher in Enschede.
1965
Royal Subsidy for Free Painting.
1967
British Council Scholarship.
Attends St. Martin's School of Art in London.
Moves to Amsterdam.
1968–present
Teaches at Ateliers '63 in Haarlem.
1971
Cassandra Foundation Award.
1973–1974
Lives and works in Rome.
1979
"Rembrandt-Preis" of the Johann Wolfgang von Goethe Stiftung in Basel.
1984–present
Professor at the Kunstakademie, Düsseldorf.
Lives and works in Amsterdam.

Selected
One-Man Exhibitions

1965
Galerie 845, Amsterdam
1967
Galerie Swart, Amsterdam
1968
Konrad Fischer, Düsseldorf
1969
Seth Siegelaub, New York
1969–1970
Audio-visuelle Dokumentationen,
Museum Haus Lange, Krefeld
1970
Galerie Yvon Lambert, Paris
1971
Galleria Sperone, Turin
Bykert Gallery, New York
Konrad Fischer, Düsseldorf
Art and Project, Amsterdam
1971–1972
Stedelijk Van Abbemuseum, Eindhoven
Galerie MTL, Brussels
1972
Galerie Yvon Lambert, Paris
Jack Wendler Gallery, London
Israel Museum, Jerusalem
Dutch Pavilion, XXXVI Venice Biennale
1972–1973
Stedelijk Museum, Amsterdam
1973
Leo Castelli Gallery, New York
Konrad Fischer, Düsseldorf
Jack Wendler Gallery, London
1974
Galleria Sperone, Turin
Konrad Fischer, Düsseldorf
Galerie Rolf Preisig, Basel
Galerie Yvon Lambert, Paris
1975
Galerie MTL, Brussels
Art and Project, Amsterdam
Cusack Gallery, Houston
Claire Copley Gallery, Los Angeles
Galleria Marilena Bonomo, Bari
Leo Castelli Gallery, New York
Kunstmuseum Luzern
1976
Scottish Arts Council, Edinburgh
Arnolfini Gallery, Bristol
Konrad Fischer, Düsseldorf
1977
Unit Gallery Chapter Arts Centre, Cardiff
Museum of Modern Art, Oxford

1978
Leo Castelli Gallery, New York
Galerie Charles Kriwin, Brussels
1979
INK, Zürich
Konrad Fischer, Düsseldorf
1980
Stedelijk Van Abbemuseum, Eindhoven
Kunsthalle, Bern
ARC Musée d'art moderne
de la ville de Paris
Galerie Yvon Lambert, Paris
Bonnefantenmuseum, Maastricht
1981
Christian Stein, Turin
Locus Solus, Genoa
1982
Anthony d'Offay, London
Abbaye de Sénanque, Gordes
Kamakura Gallery, Tokyo
1983
Karen and Jean Bernier, Athens
Leo Castelli Gallery, New York
1984
Het Gewad, Ghent
Waddington Galleries, London
1985
Galerie Maeght Lelong, Paris
Muzej Savremene Umetnosti, Belgrade
Galerija Suvremene Sumjetnosti, Zagreb

Selected Group Exhibitions

1967
*Dies alles Herzchen wird einmal
Dir gehören.* Galerie Loehr, Frankfurt
1969
Earth Art. Cornell University,
Ithaca, New York
July/August/September.
Seth Siegelaub, New York
Konzeption-Conception. Städtisches
Museum, Leverkusen
Op losse schroeven.
Stedelijk Museum, Amsterdam
Prospect '69. Kunsthalle, Düsseldorf
When Attitudes Become Form.
Kunsthalle, Bern
1970
Information.
The Museum of Modern Art, New York
1971
Guggenheim International Exhibition.
Solomon R. Guggenheim Museum,
New York
1972
Dokumenta V. Kassel
1973
Art in Space: Some Turning Points.
The Detroit Institute of Arts
1973–1974
Contemporanea. Rome
1974
Eight Contemporary Artists.
The Museum of Modern Art, New York
1977
*Europe in the Seventies: Aspects of
Recent Art.* The Art Institute of Chicago
1979
*European Dialogue: The Third Biennale
of Sydney.* The Art Gallery of New South
Wales, Sydney
1980
Explorations in the 70's.
Pittsburgh Plan for Art
1981
Westkunst. Zeitgenössische Kunst seit
1939 organized by the Museums of Cologne
1982
Dokumenta VII. Kassel
1983
17th Biennale. São Paulo
Ars '83. The Art Museum of the
Ateneum, Helsinki

1984
Toyama Now. A New Map of a New Art.
The Museum of Modern Art, Toyama
1984–1985
La Grande Parade.
Stedelijk Museum, Amsterdam
1985
Ouverture. Castello di Rivoli, Turin
Carnegie International. Museum of Art,
Carnegie Institute, Pittsburgh

Selected Bibliography

Catalogues

Ammann, Jean-Christophe. *Jan Dibbets, Autumn Melody*. Lucerne: Kunstmuseum Luzern, 1975.

Denegri, Ješa and Vos, M.M.M. *Jan Dibbets*. Belgrade: Muzej Savremene Umetnosti, 1985.

Fuchs, R.H. and Leering, J. *Jan Dibbets*. Eindhoven: Stedelijk Van Abbemuseum, 1971.

Fuchs, R.H. *Jan Dibbets*. Venice: XXXVI Biennale, 1972.

____. "Address in Honour of Mr. Jan Dibbets," *Rembrandt-Preis*. Basel: Johann Wolfgang von Goethe Stiftung, 1979.

____. *Jan Dibbets*. Eindhoven: Stedelijk Van Abbemuseum, 1980. (catalogue raisonné)

Grevenstein, Alexander van. *Bonnefanten/Saenredam, Jan Dibbets.* Maastricht: Bonnefantenmuseum, n.d.

Reise, Barbara and Vos, M.M.M. *Jan Dibbets*. Edinburgh: Scottish Arts Council Gallery, 1976.

Saenredam Sénanque Jan Dibbets 1980–1981. Gordes: Renault recherches Art et Industrie, Centre Internationale de Création Artistique, Abbaye de Sénanque, n.d. Short texts by M.M.M. Vos, Micheline Renard and Georges Duby.

Wilde, E. de, Dippel, Rini and Vos, M.M.M. *Jan Dibbets*. Amsterdam: Stedelijk Museum, 1972.

Wember, Paul. *Jan Dibbets: Audio-visuelle Dokumentationen*. Krefeld: Museum Haus Lange, 1969.

Catalogues of Group Shows

Ammann, Jean-Christophe and Brown, David. *Europe in the Seventies: Aspects of Recent Art*. Chicago: The Art Institute of Chicago, 1977.

Wat Amsterdam Betreft . . . (As Far as Amsterdam Goes . . .). Amsterdam: Stedelijk Museum, 1985. With an essay on Dibbets by Wim Beeren.

Bourdon, David. *(photo) (photo)^2 . . . (photo)^n: Sequenced Photographs*. College Park: The University of Maryland Art Gallery, 1975.

European Dialogue: The Third Biennale of Sydney. Sydney: The Art Gallery of New South Wales, 1979.

Licht, Jennifer. *Eight Contemporary Artists*. New York: The Museum of Modern Art, 1974.

Pacquement, Alfred. *Murs*. Paris: Centre Georges Pompidou, Musée nationale d'art moderne, 1981.

20 jaar verzamelen–20 Years of Art Collecting. Amsterdam: Stedelijk Museum, 1984. Compiled by Joop M. Joosten.

By Dibbets

"Laten we Zeggen . . .," Amsterdam: Galerie Swart, 1966.

Bulletin 15, Amsterdam: Art & Project, 1969.

"Send the right page . . .," *Studio International*, 180, July/August 1970, pp. 41–44.

Robin Redbreast's Territory/Sculpture 1969. Cologne: König; New York: Seth Siegelaub, 1970.

Bulletin 36, Amsterdam: Art & Project, 1971.

Bulletin 56, Amsterdam: Art & Project, 1972.

Articles

Ammann, Jean-Christophe. "Letter from Switzerland," *Art International*, 13, May 1969, pp. 48–49.

Baker, Elizabeth C. [review], *Art News*, 72, April 1973, p. 82.

Blotcamp, Carel. "Notities over het werk van Jan Dibbets," *Museumjournaal*, Stedelijk Museum, Amsterdam, 16, July 1971, pp. 139–144.

Boice, Bruce. "Jan Dibbets: The Photograph and the Photographed," *Artforum*, 11, April 1973, pp. 45–49.

Celant, Germano. "La Natura é insorta," *Casabella*, 339–340, August/September 1969, pp. 104–107.

Domingo, Willis. [review], *Arts Magazine*, 45, June 1971, pp. 52–53.

Fuchs, R.H. "Modes of Visual Experience: New Works by Jan Dibbets," *Studio International*, 185, January 1973, p. 37.

_____. "Jan Dibbets, Arnolfini, Bristol," *Art Monthly*, 3, December/January 1976/77, p. 24.

Graevenitz, Antje von. "The Art of Discovering Conflicts in Perception," *Data*, 3, Summer 1973, p. 107.

Groot, Paul. "Jan Dibbets, 'Saenredam-Sénanque'," *Artforum*, 20, Summer 1982, pp. 94–95.

Honnef, Klaus. "Audio-visuelle Dokumentationen," *Das Kunstwerk*, 23, February/March 1970, pp. 76–77.

"Interview with Jan Dibbets," *Avalanche*, Fall 1970, pp. 33–39.

Kingsley, April. [review], *Art International*, 17, May 1973, pp. 59–60.

Lebeer, Irmeline. "Jan Dibbets," *Chroniques de l'art vivant*, 31, 1972.

Mayer, Rosemary. [review], *Arts Magazine*, 47, April 1973, p. 75.

Morris, Lynda. "Jan Dibbets at Jack Wendler Gallery, London," *Studio International*, 187, January 1974, pp. 39–40.

Piller, Micky. "Jan Dibbets, Van Abbemuseum Eindhoven," *Artforum*, 18, May 1980, pp. 88–89.

Reise, Barbara. "Notes[1] on Jan Dibbets's[2] Contemporary[3] Nature[4] of Realistic[5] Classicism[6] in the Dutch[7] Tradition[8]," *Studio International*, 183, June 1972, pp. 248–255.

_____. "Jan Dibbets: A Perspective Correction," *Art News*, 71, Summer 1972, pp. 38–41.

Sheffield, Margaret. [review], *Studio International*, 191, January/February 1976, pp. 72–73.

Stimson, Paul. "Jan Dibbets at Castelli downtown," *Art in America*, 64, January/February 1976, p. 103.

Townsend, Charlotte. "Jan Dibbets in Conversation with Charlotte Townsend," *Artscanada*, 28, August/September 1971, pp. 49–50.

Tuyl, Gijs van. "Het werk van Jan Dibbets op de Biënnale van Venetië," *Museumjournaal*, Stedelijk Museum, Amsterdam, 4, 1972.

Vos, M.M.M. "Some Work of Jan Dibbets," *Flash Art*, 38, January 1973, p. 18.

Welish, Marjorie. "Jan Dibbets at Castelli," *Art in America*, 71, November 1983, p. 225.

Wooster, Ann Sargent. [review], *Artforum*, 14, January 1976, pp. 69–70.

Lenders to the Exhibition

Bayer USA Inc.
Bonnefantenmuseum, Maastricht
Castello di Rivoli, Turin
Daled Collection
Mr. and Mrs. Robert J. Dodds III
Exxon Corporation
Margaret H. Van Wylick-Froelicher
Sondra and Charles Gilman Jr.
Solomon R. Guggenheim Museum,
    New York
Haags Gemeentemuseum
Hamburger Kunsthalle
Vance E. Kondon and
    Liesbeth Giesberger
Kröller-Müller Museum, Otterlo,
    loan from Geert-Jan Visser
Louisiana Museum of Modern Art,
    Humlebaek
Morton G. Neumann Family Collection
Panza di Biumo Collection
Mrs. B. De Poorter
Rolf Preisig
Hannelore B. Schulhof
Joan S. Sonnabend
Stedelijk Museum, Amsterdam
Trustees of the Tate Gallery, London
Mrs. Hester van Royen
Von der Heydt-Museum der Stadt Wuppertal
Walker Art Center, Minneapolis
Mike and Penny Winton
Mr. and Mrs. H. Wyss
and four private collections

Acknowledgments

In 1978 the Walker Art Center acquired a large panoramic landscape by Jan Dibbets: *Horizon 1°–10° Land,* a 1973 composition of slatlike vertical photographic images of a distant landscape. In the ensuing years, Dibbets and I met a number of times in his Amsterdam studio and during his visits to Minneapolis to discuss the possibility of an exhibition of his work to be organized by the Walker Art Center. As our friendship developed so did our plans for a major American retrospective of his production. From the outset Jan Dibbets was extremely helpful in identifying key works for inclusion in this exhibition and he willingly submitted to the Walker staff's many questions concerning the origins of his themes and stylistic approaches.

This overview of his landscape and architectural images from the mid–1960s to the present has been an international effort. Fortunately, we were able to enlist the collaboration of several of Dibbets's friends in Holland to help realize this project. Particularly important was the participation of Rudi Fuchs, the Director of the Stedelijk Van Abbemuseum in Eindhoven, whose knowledge of Dibbets's art is equaled by his consistent support of it through exhibitions he has arranged. For the catalogue of this exhibition, Fuchs has provided a thoughtful analysis of Dibbets's stylistic development. The distinguished Amsterdam-based art historian Marcel Vos has contributed revealing observations on Dibbets's use of photography. Vos's essay was beautifully translated by Ina Rike. The talents of Margriet Suren, previously on the staff of the Van Abbemuseum and now a free-lance scholar, were indispensable in locating and helping to secure loans of Dibbets's work in European collections and in gathering and organizing the illustrations for this book. Coordinating many details of preparing the exhibition in Holland was Hendrik Driessen, Deputy Director of the Van Abbemuseum, assisted by Bert de Graaf.

While many members of the Walker Art Center staff were directly involved in the exhibition's preparation, particular thanks are due Stephen Fleischman, Director of Program Planning, and Donna Harkavy, Curatorial Assistant, who oversaw many details of its production. Initial planning for the exhibition was carried out in 1985 by the then Chief Curator of Walker Art Center, Robert Murdock, and now Program Director of the IBM Gallery of Science and Art in New York. The preparation and editing of the catalogue were the responsibility of Mildred Friedman, Design Curator. The catalogue was designed by Jeffrey Cohen. Assisting in the preparation of its manuscript were Martha Limburg and Linda Krenzin; and the Walker Art Center's role in shipment and circulation of the exhibition was handled by Sharon Howell, Associate Registrar.

Finally, we are extremely grateful to the many private and institutional lenders in Europe and the United States who have so generously made their works by Jan Dibbets available for the extensive tour of this exhibition.

Martin Friedman, Director

Travel Schedule

Solomon R. Guggenheim Museum
New York, New York
11 September to 1 November 1987

Walker Art Center
Minneapolis, Minnesota
17 January to 27 March 1988

The Detroit Institute of Arts
Detroit, Michigan
24 April to 19 June 1988

Norton Gallery and School of Art
West Palm Beach, Florida
30 July to 2 October 1988

Stedelijk Van Abbemuseum
Eindhoven, The Netherlands
6 November 1988 to 1 January 1989

153

Index of Illustrations

Photo Credits